Notes of a Camp-Follower on the Western

Ernest William Hornung was born in Middlesbrough, England on youngest of eight children.

Although spending most of his life in England and France he spent two years in Australia from 1884 and that experience was to colour and influence much of his written works.

His most famous character A. J. Raffles, 'the gentleman thief', was published first in Cassell's Magazine during 1898 and was to make him famous across the world as the new century dawned.

Hornung also wrote several stage plays and was a gifted poet.

Spending time with the troops in WWI he published Notes of a Camp-Follower on the Western Front during 1919, a detailed account of his time there. This was especially close to his heart as his son, and only child, was killed at the Second Battle of Ypres on 6th July 1915.

Ernest William Hornung died in Saint-Jean-de-Luz, in the south of France on 22nd March 1921.

Index of Contents

AN ARK IN THE MUD

UNDER WAY

'There's our hut!' said the young hut-leader, pointing through iron palings at a couple of toy Noah's Arks built large. 'No—that's the nth Division's cinema. The Y.M.C.A. is the one beyond.'

The enclosure behind the palings had been a parade-ground in piping times; and British squads, from the pink French barracks outside the gates, still drilled there between banks of sterilised rubbish and lagoons of unmedicated mud. The place was to become familiar to me under many aspects. I have known it more than presentable in a clean suit of snow, and really picturesque with a sharp moon cocked upon some towering trees, as yet strangely intact. It was at its best, perhaps, as a nocturne pricked out by a swarm of electric torches, going and coming along the duck-boards in a grand chain of sparks and flashes. But its true colours were the wet browns and drabs of that first glimpse in the December dusk, with the Ark hull down in the mud, and the cinema a sister ship across her bows.

The hut-leader ushered me on board with the courtesy of a young commander inducting an elderly new mate; the difference was that I had all the ropes to learn, with the possible exception of one he had already shown me on our way from the local headquarters of the Y.M.C.A. The battered town was full of English soldiers, to whom indeed it owed its continued existence on the right side of the Line. In the gathering twilight, and the deeper shade of beetling ruins, most of them saluted either my leader's British warm, or my own voluminous trench-coat (with fleece lining), on the supposition of officers within. Left to myself, I should have done the wrong thing every time. It is expressly out of order for a camp-follower to give or take salutes. Yet what is he to do, when he gets a beauty from one whose boots he is unfit to black? My leader had been showing me, with a pleasant nod and a genial civilian gesture, easier to emulate than to acquire.

In the hut he left me to my own investigations while he was seeing to his lamps. The round stove in the centre showed a rosy chimney through the gloom, like a mast in a ship's saloon; and in the two half-lights the place looked scrupulously swept and garnished for our guests, a number of whom were already waiting outside for us to open. The trestle tables, with nothing on them but a dusky polish, might have been mathematically spaced, each with a pair of forms in perfect parallels, and nothing else but a piano and an under-sized billiard-table on all the tidy floor. The usual display of bunting, cheap but cheerful, hung as banners from the joists, a garish vista from platform to counter. Behind the counter were the shelves of shimmering goods, biscuits and candles in open cases on the floor, and as many exits as a scene in a farce. One door led into our room: an oblong cabin with camp beds for self and leader, tables covered with American cloth, dust, toilet requisites, more dust, candle-grease and tea-things, and a stove of its own in roseate blast like the one down the hut.

The crew of two orderlies lived along a little passage in their kitchen, and were now at their tea on packing-cases by the boiler fire. They were both like Esau hairy men, with very little of the soldier left about them. Their unlovely beds were the principal pieces of kitchen furniture. In the kitchen, too, for obscure reasons not for me to investigate, were the washing arrangements for all hands, and any face or neck that felt inclined. I had heard a whisper of Officers' Baths in the vicinity; it came to mind like the tinkle of a brook at these discoveries.

At 4.30 the unkempt couple staggered in with the first urn, and I took my post at the tap. One of them shuffled down the hut to open up; our young skipper stuck a carriage candle in its grease on the edge of the counter, over his till, saying he was as short of paraffin as of change; and into the half-lit gloom marched a horde of determined soldiers, and so upon the counter and my urn in double file. 'Tea, please, sir!' 'Two teas!' 'Coop o' tay, plase!' The accents were from every district I had ever known, and were those of every class, including the one that has no accent at all. They warmed the blood like a medley of patriotic airs, and I commenced potman as it were to martial music.

It was, perhaps, the least skilled labour to be had in France, but that evening it was none too light. Every single customer began with tea: the mugs flew through my hands as fast as I could fill them, until my end of the counter swam in livid pools, and the tilted urn was down to a gentle dribble. Now was the chance to look twice at the consumers of our innocuous blend. One had a sheaf of wound-stripes on his sleeve; another was fresh trench-mud from leathern jerkin (where my view of him began) to the crown of his shrapnel helmet; many wore the bonnets of a famous Scotch Division, all were in their habit as they fought; and there they were waiting for their tea, a long perspective of patient faces, like school-children at a treat. And here was I, fairly launched upon the career which a facetious density has summed up as 'pouring out tea and prayer in equal parts,' and prepared to continue with the first half of the programme till further orders: the other was less in my line—but I could have poured out a fairly fluent thanksgiving for the atmosphere of youth and bravery, and most infectious vitality, which already filled the hut.

In the meantime there was much to be learnt from my seasoned neighbour at the till, and to admire in his happy control of gentlemen on their way up the Line. Should they want more matches than it suited him to sell, then want must be their master; did some sly knave appear at the top of the queue, without having worked his way up past my urn, then it was: 'I saw you, Jock! Go round and come up in your turn!' Or was it a man with no change, and was there hardly any in the till?—'Take two steps to the rear, my friend, and when I have the change I'll serve you!' When he had the change, the sparks might have flown with it through his fingers; he was lightning calculator and conjuror in one, knew the foul franc note of a dubious bank with less than half an eye, and how to refuse it with equal firmness and good-humour. I hardly knew whether to feel hurt or flattered at being perpetually 'Mr.' to this natural martinet, my junior it is true by decades, but a leader I was already proud to follow and obey.

In the first lull he deserted me in order to make tea in our room, but took his with the door open, shouting out the price of aught I had to sell with an endearing verve, name and prefix included every time. It made me feel more than ever like the mate of a ship, and anxious to earn my certificate.

Then I had my tea—with the door shut—and already an aching back for part of the fun. For already the whole thing was my idea of fun—the picnic idea—an old weakness. Huts especially were always near my heart, and our room in this one reminded me of bush huts adored for their discomfort in my teens. Of the two I preferred the bush fireside, a hearth like a powder-closet and blazing logs; but candles in their own grease-spots were an improvement on the old slush-lamp of moleskin and mutton-fat. The likeness reached its height in the two sheetless bunks, but there it ended. Not a sound was a sound ever heard before. The continual chink of money in the till outside; the movement of many feet, trained not to shuffle; the constant coughing of men otherwise in superhuman health; the crude tinkle of the piano at the far end of the hut—the efficient pounding of the cinema piano—the screw-like throb of their petrol engine—the periodical bringing-down of their packed house, no doubt by the ubiquitous Mr. Chaplin! Those were the sounds to which we took our tea in the state-room of the Ark. She might have been on a pleasure-trip all the time.

That first night I remember going back and diving into open cases of candles, and counting out packets of cigarettes and biscuits, sticks of chocolate, boxes of matches, and reaching down tinned salmon, sardines, boot-laces, boot-polish, shaving-soap and tooth-paste, button-sticks, 'sticks of lead' (otherwise pencils), writing-pads, Nosegay Shag, Royal Seal, or twist if we had it, and shouting for the prices as I went, coping with the change by light of luck and nature, but doling out the free stationery with a base lingering relief, until my back was a hundred and all the silver of the allied realms one composite coin that danced without jingling in the till. Gold stripes meant nothing to me now; shrapnel helmets were as high above me as the stars; the only hero was the man who didn't want change. Often in the early part I thought the queue was coming to an end; it was always the sign for a fresh influx; and when the National Anthem came thumping from the cinema, the original Ark might have sunk under such a boarding-party of thirsty tea-drinkers as we had still to receive. I noted that they called it tea regardless of the contents of the urn, which changed first to coffee and then to cocoa as the night wore on: tea was the generic term.

At last the smarter and tarter of the two orderlies, he who compounded the contents of the urns, sidled without ceremony to the commander's elbow.

'It wants a minute to the 'alf-hour, sir.'

Gramophone alone could give the husky tone of chronic injury, palette and brush the red eyes of resentment turned upon his kind beyond the counter. Our leader consulted his wrist-watch with a brisk gesture.

'I'll serve the next six men,' he ultimated, and the seventh man knocked at his heart in vain. Green curtains closed the counter in the wistful faces of the rest; if I can see them still, it is the heavenly music of those curtain-rings that I hear! The mind's eye peeps through once more, and spies the last gobblers at the splashed tables littered with mugs and empty tins; the last dawdlers on a floor ankle-deep in the envelopes of twopenny and half-franc packets of biscuits; and a little man broom-in-hand at the open door, spoiling to sweep all the lot into outer darkness.

In the kitchen, while both orderlies fell straight to work upon this Augean scene, our versatile leader, as little daunted by the hour, gave further expression to his personality in an omelette worthy of the country, and in lashings of Suchard cocoa made with a master hand. I remember with much gratitude that he also made my yawning bed, and that we turned in early to the tune of rain:

A fusillade upon the roof, A tattoo on the pane.

Only the pane was canvas, and the fusillade accompanied by some local music from the guns outside the town.

As 'the true love-story commences at the altar,' so the real work of a hut only begins at the counter. You may turn out to be the disguised prince of salesmen, and yet fail to deliver the goods that really matter. I am not thinking of 'goody' goods at all, but of the worker's personality such as it may be. It is not more essential for an actor to 'get across the footlights' than it is for the Y.M.C.A. counter-jumper to start by clearing that obstacle, and mixing with the men for all he can show himself to be worth.

The Ark was such a busy canteen that all this is easier said than it was done. Every morning we were kept at it as continuously from eleven to one as ever we were from four-thirty to eight-thirty. Those were our business hours; and though it was never quite such fierce shopping in the forenoon, it was then that the leader would go off in quest of fresh supplies and I was apt to be left in charge. This happened my very first morning. Shall I ever forget the intimidating multitude of Army boots seen under the door before we opened! And there was another of the early days, when the Somersets stormed our parapet in full fighting paraphernalia, with only me to stand up to them. Not much chance of foregathering then; but never an hour, seldom a single transaction within the hour, but brought me from the other side some quaint remark, some adorable display of patience, courtesy, or homely fun. The change difficulty was chronic, and mutually most exasperating; it was over that stile the men were always helping each other or helping me, with never a trace of the irritation I felt myself. They were the most delightful customers one could wish to serve. But that made it the more tantalising to have but a word with them on business. My young chief was once more my better here; he had only to be behind the counter to 'get across' as much as he liked, and in as few words. But I required a slack half-hour when I could take my pipe down the hut and seek out some solitary, or make overtures to the man at the piano.

It was generally the man's chum who responded in the first instance; for every Æneas in the new legions has his staunch Achates, who collects the praise as for the firm, adding his own mite in a beaming whisper. 'He has his own choir in Edinburgh,' said one Jock of another who was playing and singing the Scottish songs with urgent power. The piano is the surest touchstone in a hut. It brings out the man of talent—but also the bore who hammers with one thick-skinned finger—but also the prevailing lenience that puts up with the bore. I have been entreated to keep my piano locked and the key in the till; and once on the counter I found an anonymous notice, with a line requesting me to affix it to the instrument without delay: 'If you do play, do play—If you don't play, don't!' But a pianist of any pretensions has a crowd round him in a minute; and a splendid little audience it always is. The set concert, as I heard it, was not a patch on these unpremeditated recitals.

One night the hut was full of Riflemen, one of whom was strumming away to his own contentment, but with only the usual trusty chum for audience. I brought my pipe to the other side of the piano, and the performer got up and talked across to me for nearly an hour. He was a dark little garrulous fellow of no distinction, and he talked best with his eyes upon the keyboard, but the chum's broad grin of eager admiration never ceased to ply between us. The little Rifleman had borne a charmed life indeed, especially on Passchendaele Ridge, the scene of his latest misadventures. He was as idiomatic as Ortheris in his generation, but I only remember: 'I looked a fair Bairnsfather, not 'alf!' He was the nearest approach to a 'Bairnsfather' I ever encountered in the flesh, but the compliment to the draughtsman is no smaller for that. A third Rifleman, less demonstratively uncritical than the chum, joined the party; and at the end I ventured to ask all three in turn what they had been doing before the war.

'I,' said the little man, 'was a house-painter at Crewe.'

'And I,' said the grinning chum, 'was conductor of a 28 motor-'bus. I expect we've often dropped you at the Y.M.C.A. in Tottenham Court Road, sir.'

'And you?'—I turned to the last comer—'if it isn't a rude question?'

'Oh, I,' said he, with the pride that would conceal itself, 'I'm in the building line. But I operate a bioscope at night!'

The historic present put his attitude in a nutshell. He might have been operating that bioscope the night before, be due back the next, and just having a look at things in France on his night off. His expert eye was not perceptibly impressed with the spectacle of war as he was seeing it off the films; but the house-painter seemed to be making the most of his long holiday from house-painting, and my old friend the conductor did not sigh in my hearing for his 28.

I took the party back with me to the counter, where they honoured me by partaking of cocoa and biscuits as my guests. It was all there was to do for three such hardy and mature philosophers; and I never saw or heard of them again, long as their cap-badge set me looking for one or other of their pleasant faces underneath. It was always rather sad when we had made friends with a man who never came near us again. In times of heavy fighting it was no wonder, but in the winter it seemed in the nature of a black mark against the hut.

There were two other Riflemen who were in that night, and hit me harder in a softer spot. They were both tragically young, one of them a pretty boy in a muffler that might have been knitted by any mother in the land. They were not enjoying their war, these two, but they smiled none the less as they let it out; they had come in of their own free will, as soon as ever their tender years allowed, and survived all the carnage of the Somme and of Passchendaele. They could afford to smile; but they had also outlived their romantic notions of a war, and were too young to bear it willingly in any other spirit. They had honest shudders for the horrors they had seen, and they frankly loathed going back into the mud or ice of the December trenches.

'Every time,' said the pretty boy, as they took cocoa with me, 'it seems worse.'

'But for the Y.M.C.A.,' said the other, with simple feeling, 'I believe I should have gone mad.'

That was something to hear. But what was there to say to such a pair? One had been a clerk in Huddersfield; the other, a shade less gentle, but, to equalise the appeal, an only child, foreman of some works in Derbyshire. Indubitably they were both wishing themselves back in their old situations; but equally without a doubt they were both still proud of the act of sacrifice which had brought them to this. The last was the frame of mind to recall by hook or crook. One can be proud of such boys, even if their spirit is not all it was, and so perhaps make them prouder of themselves; the hard case is the man who waited for compulsion, who has no old embers of loyalty or enterprise to coax into a modest flame. This type takes a lot of waking up, and yet, like other heavy sleepers, once awake may do as well as any.

At the foot of our hut, beyond piano, billiard-table, and platform (only the case the billiard-table had come in), was the Quiet Room in which the men were entitled to read and write without interruption. One of those first nights I peeped in there with my pipe, at a moment of fourfold psychology.

In one corner two men were engaged in some form of violent prayer or intercession; not on their knees, but seated side by side. One, and he much the younger of the two, appeared to be wrestling for the other's soul, to be at all but physical grips with some concrete devil of his inner vision; at any rate he was making a noise that entirely destroyed the character of our Quiet Room. But the other occupants, so far from complaining, seemed equally wrapped up in their own affairs, and oblivious to the pother. The third man was writing a tremendous letter, at great speed, face and hands and flying pencil strongly lighted by a candle-end almost under his nose, more shame for our poor lamplight! The fourth and last of the party, a good-looking Guardsman with a puzzled frown, poising the pencil of an unready scribe, at once invoked my aid in another form of literary enterprise. He was making his will in his field pocket-book; could I tell him how to spell the pretty name of one of his little daughters? Would I mind looking it all over, and seeing if it would do?

'Going up the Line for the first time on Tuesday,' he explained, 'and it's as well to be prepared.'

He was perfectly calm about it. He had thought of everything; his wife, I remember, was to have 'the float and the two horses, to do the best she can with'; but the little girls were specifically remembered, and the identity of each clinched by their surname after the one that took more spelling. A dairyman, I imagined from his mild phlegmatic face; but it seemed he was the village butcher somewhere in Leicestershire. His date of enrolment bespoke either the conscript or the eleventh-hour volunteer, and his sad air made me decide which in my own mind. He had obviously no stomach for the trenches, but on the other hand he showed no fear. It was the kind of passive courage I longed to fan into enthusiasm, but knew I never could. I am glad I had not the impertinence to try. Two or three weeks later, I found myself serving a delightfully gay and jaunty Guardsman, in whom I suddenly recognised my friend.

'Come back all right, then?' I could only say.

'Rather!' said he, with schoolboy gusto. He was another being; the trenches themselves had wrought the change. I would not put a V.C. past that butcher if he is still alive, or past any other tardy patriot for that matter. Patriotism is a ray of inner light, and may never even come to a glow of carnal courage; on the other hand, it is the greatest mistake to impute cowardice to the shirker. Selfishness is oftener the restraining power, insensibility oftener still. After all, even in the officer class, it was not everybody who could see that personal considerations ceased to exist on the day war broke out. This busy butcher had been a fine man all the time, and not unnaturally taken up with the price of sheep, the tricks of the weather, the wife and the little girls. May the float and the two horses yet be his to drive more furiously than of old!

A few nights later still, and the pretty ex-clerk was smiling through his collar of soft muffler across the counter. He, too, had made his tour without disaster, or as much discomfort as he feared, and so had his chum the whilom foreman. These reunions were always a delight to me, sometimes a profound reassurance and relief. But those first three jolly Riflemen had vanished from my ken, and I wish I knew their fate.

SUNDAY ON BOARD

I see from my diary it was on a Sunday night I found that memorable quartette so diversely employed in our Quiet Room. So, after all, there had been something to lead up to the most singular feature of the scene. Sunday is Sunday in a Y.M.C.A. hut, and in ours it was no more a day of rest than it is in any regular place of worship; for that is exactly what we were privileged to provide for a very famous Division whose headquarters were then in our immediate neighbourhood.

Overnight the orderlies would work late arranging the chairs church-fashion, moving the billiard-table, and preparing the platform for a succession of morning services. These might begin with a celebration of the Holy Communion at nine, to be followed by a C. of E. parade service at ten and one for mixed Nonconformists, or possibly for Presbyterians only, at eleven; the order might be reversed, and the opening celebration was not inevitable; but the preparations were the same for all denominations and all degrees of ceremonial.

In a secular sense the hut was closed all morning. But in our private precincts those Sabbaths were not so easy to observe. The free forenoon was too good a chance to count the week's takings, amounting in a busy canteen like ours to several thousand francs; this took even a quick hand all his time, what with the small foul notes that first defied the naked eye, and then fell to shreds between the fingers; and often have I watched my gay young leader, his confidence ruffled by an alien frown, slaving like a miser between a cross-fire of stentorian hymns. For the cinema, ever our rival, was in similar request between the same hours; and we were lucky if the selfsame hymn, in different keys and stages, did not smite simultaneously upon either ear.

On a Sunday afternoon we opened at four instead of half-past, and drove a profane trade as merrily as in the week until the hut service at six-thirty. During service the counter was closed; and after service, in our hut, we drew a firm line at tea and biscuits for what was left of the working night.

Neither of ourselves being ordained of any denomination, we as a rule requisitioned one of the many ministers among the Y.M.C.A. workers in our district to preach the sermon and offer up the prayers: almost invariably he was the shepherd of some Nonconformist fold at home, and a speaker born or made. But the men themselves set matters going, congregating at the platform end and singing hymns—their favourite hymns—not many of them mine—for a good half-hour before the pastor was due to appear. Of course, only a proportion of those present joined in; but it was a surprising proportion; and the uncritical forbearance of those who did not take part used to impress me quite as much as the unflinching fervour of those who did. But then it is not too soon to say that in all my months in an Army area I never once saw or heard Religion, in any shape or form, flouted by look or word.

The hymns were always started by the same man, a spectacled N.C.O. in a Red Cross unit, with a personality worthy of his stripes. I think he must have been a street preacher before the war; at any rate he used to get leave to hold a service of his own on Tuesday evenings, and I have listened to his sermon more than once. Indeed, it was impossible not to listen, every rasping word of the uncompromising harangue being more than audible at our end of the hut, no matter what we were doing. The man had an astounding flow of spiritual invective, at due distance the very drum-fire of withering anathema, but sorry stuff of a familiar order at close range. It was impossible not to respect this red-hot gospeller, who knew neither fear nor doubt, nor the base art of mincing words; and he had a strong following among the men, who seemed to enjoy his onslaughts, whether they took them to heart or not. But I liked him better on a Sunday evening, when his fiery spirit was content to 'warm the stage' for some meek minister by a preliminary service of right hearty song.

But those ministers were wonders in their way; not a man of them so meek upon the platform, nor one but had the knack of fluent, pointed, and courageous speech. They spoke without notes, from the break of the platform, like tight-sleeved conjurors; and they spoke from their hearts to many that beat the faster for their words. In that congregation there were no loath members; only those who liked need sit and listen; the rest were free to follow their own devices, within certain necessary limitations. The counter, to be sure, had those green curtains drawn across it for the nonce. But all at that end of the hut were welcome as ever to their game of draughts, their cigarettes and newspapers, even their murmur of conversation. It generally happened, however, that the murmur died away as the preacher warmed to his work, and the bulk of the address was followed in attentive silence by all present. I used to think this a greater than any pulpit triumph ever won; and when it was all over, and the closing hymn had been sung with redoubled fervour, a knot of friendly faces would waylay the minister on his passage up the hut.

And yet how much of his success was due to the sensitive response of these simple-hearted, uncomplaining travellers in the valley of Death! No work of man is easier to criticise than a sermon, no sort of criticism cheaper or maybe in poorer taste; and yet I have felt, with all envy of their gift and their sincerity, that even these powerful preachers were, many of them, missing their great opportunity, missing the obvious point. Morality was too much their watchword, Sin the too frequent burden of their eloquence. It is not as sinners that we should view the men who are fighting for us in the great war against international sin. They are soldiers of Christ if ever such drew sword; then let them contemplate the love of Christ, and its human reflex in their own heroic hearts, not the cleft in the hoof of all who walk this earth! That, and the grateful love we also bear them, who cannot fight ourselves, seem to me the gist of war-time Christianity: that, and the immortality of the soul they may be rendering up at any moment for our sake and for His.

It is hateful to think of these great men in the light of their little sins. What thistledown to weigh against their noble sacrifice! Yet there are those who expatiate on soldiers' sins as though the same men had never committed any in their unregenerate civil state, before putting hand to the redemption of the world; who would charge every frailty to the war's account, as if vice had not flourished, to common knowledge and the despair of generations, in idyllic villages untouched by any previous war, and run like a poisoned vein through all the culture of our towns. The point is not that the worst has still to be eradicated out of poor human nature, but that the best as we know it now is better than the best we dared to dream in happier days.

Such little sins as they denounce, and ask to be forgiven in the sinner's name! Bad language, for one; as if the low thoughtless word should seriously belittle the high deliberate deed! The decencies of language let us by all manner of means observe, but as decencies, not as virtues without which a man shall not enter the Kingdom of Heaven. Taste is the bed-rock of this matter, and what is harmless at one's own fireside might well empty a public hall and put the police in possession. To stigmatise mere coarseness of speech as a first-class sin is to defeat an admirable end by the unwitting importation of a false yet not unnatural glamour.

The thing does matter, because the modern soldier is less 'full of strange oaths' than of certain façons de parler which must not be suffered to pass into the currency of the village ale-house after the war. They are base coin, very; but still the primary offence is against manners, not morals; and public opinion, not pulpit admonition, is the thing to put it down.

In a Y.M.C.A. hut the wise worker will not hear very much more than he is meant to hear; but there are times when only a coward or a fool would hold his own tongue, and that is when an ounce of tact is worth a ton of virtue. It is well to consider every minute what the men are going through, how entirely the refining influence of their womankind has passed out of their lives, and how noticeably far from impropriety are the thoughts that clothe themselves in this grotesque and hateful habit of speech.

Let me close a tender topic with the last word thereon, as spoken by a Canadian from Vimy Ridge, who came into my hut (months later, when I had one of my own) but slightly sober, yet more so than his friends, with whom remonstrance became imperative.

'I say! I say!' one had to call down from the counter. 'The language is getting pretty thick down there!'

'Beg pardon, sir. Very sorry,' said my least inebriated friend, at once; then, after a moment's thought— 'But the shells is pretty thick where we come from!'

It was a better answer than he knew.

CHRISTMAS UP THE LINE

UNDER FIRE

Soon the shy wintry sun was wearing a veil of frosted silver. The eye of the moon was on us early in the afternoon, ever a little wider open and a degree colder in its stare. All one day our mud rang like an anvil to the tramp of rubicund customers in greatcoats and gloves; and the next day they came and went like figures on the film next-door, silent and outstanding upon a field of dazzling snow.

But behind the counter we had no such seasonable sights to cheer us; behind the counter, mugs washed overnight needed wrenching off their shelf, and three waistcoats were none too many. In our room, for all the stove that reddened like a schoolgirl, and all the stoking that we did last thing at night, no amount of sweaters, blankets, and miscellaneous wraps was excessive provision against the early morning. By dawn, which leant like lead against our canvas windows, and poked sticks of icy light through a dozen holes and crannies, the only unfrozen water in the hut was in the kitchen boiler and in my own hot-water bottle. I made no bones about this trusty friend; it hung all day on a conspicuous nail; and it did not prevent me from being the first up in the morning, any more than modesty shall deter me from trumpeting the fact. One of us had to get up to lay the stove and light the fire, and it was my chance of drawing approximately even with my brisk commander. No competing with his invidious energy once he had taken the deck; but here was a march I could count on stealing while he slept the sleep of the young. Often I was about before the orderlies, and have seen the two rogues lying on their backs in the dim light of their kitchen, side by side like huge dirty children. As for me, blackened and bent double by my exertions, swaddled in fleece lining and other scratch accoutrements, no doubt I looked the lion grotesque of the party; but, by the time the wood crackled and the chimney drew, I too had my inner glow.

So we reached the shortest day; then came a break, and for me the Christmas outing of a lifetime.

The Y.M.C.A. in that sector had just started an outpost of free cheer in the support line. It was a new departure for the winter only, a kind of cocoa-kitchen in the trenches, and we were all very eager to take our turn as cooks. The post was being manned by relays of the workers in our area, one at a time and for a week apiece; but at Christmas there were to be substantial additions to the nightly offering. It was the obvious thing to suggest that extra help would be required, and to volunteer for the special duty. But one may jump at such a chance and yet feel a sneaking thrill of morbid apprehension, and yet again enjoy the whole thing the more for that very feeling. Such was my case as I lit the fire on the morning of the 21st of December, foolishly wondering whether I should ever light it again. By all accounts our pitch up the Line was none too sheltered in any sense, and the severity of the weather was not the least intimidating prospect. But for forty mortal months I would have given my right eye to see trench life with my left; and I was still prepared to strike that bargain and think it cheap.

The man already on the spot was coming down to take me back with him: we met at our headquarters over the mid-day meal, by which time my romantic experience had begun. I had walked the ruined streets in a shrapnel helmet, endeavouring to look as though it belonged to me, and had worn a gas-mask long enough to hope I might never have to do so for dear life. The other man had been wearing his in a gas-alarm up the Line; he had also been missed by a sniper, coming down the trench that morning; and had much to say about a man who had not been missed, but had lain, awaiting burial, all the day before on the spot where we were to spend our Christmas ... It was three o'clock and incipient twilight when we made a start.

Our little headquarters Ford 'bus took us the first three miles, over the snow of a very famous battle-field, not a whole year old in history, to the mouth of a valley planted with our guns. Alighting here we made as short work of that valley as appearances permitted, each with a shifty eye for the next shell-hole in case of need; there were plenty of them, including some extremely late models, but it was not our lot to see the collection enlarged. Neither had our own batteries anything to say over our heads; and presently the trenches received us in fair order, if somewhat over-heated. I speak for myself and that infernal fleece lining, which I had buttoned back into its proper place. It alone precluded an indecent haste.

But in the trenches we could certainly afford to go slower, and I for one was not sorry. It was too wonderful to be in them in the flesh. They were almost just what I had always pictured them; a little narrower, perhaps; and the unbroken chain of duck-boards was a feature not definitely foreseen; and the printed sign-boards had not the expected air of a joke, might rather have been put up by order of the London County Council. But the extreme narrowness was a surprise, and indeed would have taken my breath away had I met my match in some places. An ordinary gaunt warrior caused me to lean hard against my side of the trench, and to apologise rather freely as he squeezed past; a file of them in leather jerkins, with snow on their toe-caps and a twinkle under their steel hat-brims, almost tempted me to take a short cut over the top. I wondered would I have got very far, or dropped straight back into the endless open grave of the communication trench.

Seen from afar, as I knew of old, that was exactly what the trenches looked like; but from the inside they appeared more solid and rather deeper than any grave dug for the dead. The whole thing put me more in mind of primitive ship-building—the great ribs leaning outwards—flat timbers in between—and over all sand-bags and sometimes wire-work with the precise effect of bulwarks and hammock-netting. Even the mouths of dug-outs were not unlike port-holes flush with the deck; and many a piquant glimpse we caught in passing, bits of faces lit by cigarette-ends and half-sentences or snatches of sardonic song; then the trench would twist round a corner into solitude, as a country road shakes off a hamlet, and on we trudged through the thickening dusk. Once, where the sand-bags were lower than I had noticed, I thought some very small bird had chirped behind my head, until the other man turned his and smiled.

'Hear that?' he said. 'That was a bullet! It's just about where they sniped at me this morning.'

I shortened my stick, and crept the rest of the way like the oldest inhabitant of those trenches, as perhaps I was.

CASUALTIES

It was nearly dark when our journey ended at one of those sunken roads which make a name for themselves on all battle-fields, and duly complicate the Western Front. Sometimes they cut the trench as a level crossing does a street, and then it is not a bad rule to cross as though a train were coming. Sometimes it is the trench that intersects the sunken road; this happened here. We squeezed through a gap in the sand-bags, a gap exactly like a stile in a stone fence, and from our feet the bleak road rose with a wild effect into the wintry sunset.

It was a road of some breadth, but all crinkled and misshapen in its soiled bandage of frozen snow. Palpable shell-holes met a touchy eye for them on every side; one, as clean-cut as our present footprints, literally adjoined a little low sand-bagged shelter, of much the same dimensions as a blackfellow's gunyah in the bush. This inviting habitation served as annex to a small enough hut at least three times its size; the two cowered end to end against the sunken roadside, each roof a bit of bank-top in more than camouflage, with real grass doing its best to grow in real sods.

'No,' said the other man, 'only the second half of the hut's our hut. This first half's a gum-boot store. The sand-bagged hutch at the end of all things is where we sleep.'

The three floors were sunk considerably below the level of the road, and a sunken track of duck-boards outside the semi-detached huts was like the bottom of a baby trench. We looked into our end; it was colder and darker than the open air, but cubes of packing-case and a capacious boiler took stark shape in the gloom.

'I should think we might almost start our fire,' said the other man. 'We daren't by daylight, on account of the smoke; we should have a shell on us in no time. As it is, we only get waifs and strays from their machine-guns; but one took the rim off a man's helmet, as neat as you could do it with a pair of shears, only last night out here on these duck-boards.'

Yet those duck-boards outside the hut were the next best cover to the hut itself; accordingly the men greatly preferred waiting about in the open road, which the said machine-guns could spray at pleasure on the chance of laying British dust. So I gathered from the other man: so I very soon saw for myself. Night had fallen, and at last we had lighted our boiler fire, with the help of a raw-boned orderly supplied by the battalion of Jocks then holding the front line. And the boiler fire had retaliated by smoking all three of us out of the hut.

This was an initial fiasco of each night I was there; to it I owe sights that I can still see as plain as the paper under my pen, and bits of dialogue and crashes of orchestral gun-fire, maddeningly impossible to reproduce. Are there no gramophone records of such things? If not, I make a present of the idea to those whom it officially concerns. They are as badly needed as any films, and might be more easily obtained.

The frosty moon was now nearly full, and a grey-mauve sky, wearing just the one transcendent jewel of light, as brilliant in its way as the dense blue of equatorial noon. Upon this noble slate the group of armed men, waiting about in the road above the duck-boards, was drawn in shining outline; silvered rifles slung across coppery leathern shoulders; earthenware mugs turned to silver goblets in their hands, and each tilted helmet itself a little fallen moon. A burst of gun-fire, and not a helmet turned; the rat-tat-tat of a machine-gun, but no shining shoulder twinkled with the tiniest shrug. And yet the devil's orchestra might have been tuning up at their feet, under the very stage they trod with culpable unconcern.

Two melodramatic little situations (as they seemed to me, but not to them) came about for our immediate benefit, and in appropriately quick succession as I remember them. A wounded Jock figured in each; neither was a serious case; the first one too light, it was feared, to score at all. The man did just come limping along our duck-boards, but only very slightly, though I rather think a comrade's arm played a fifth-wheel part in the proceedings. It was only a boot that had been sliced across the instep. A shoemaker's knife could not have made a cleaner job so far; but 'a bit graze on ma fut' was all the sufferer himself could claim, amid a murmur of sympathy that seemed exaggerated, ill as it became a civilian even to think so.

The other casualty was a palpable hit in the fore-arm. First aid had been applied, including an empty sand-bag as top bandage, before the wounded man appeared with his escort in the moonlight; but now there was a perverse shortage of that very commiseration which had been lavished upon the man with the wounded boot. This was a real wound, 'a Blighty one' and its own reward: the man who could time matters to so cynical a nicety with regard to Christmas, and then only 'get it in the arrum,' which notoriously means a long time rather than a bad one, was obviously not a man to be pitied. He was a person to be plied with the driest brand of North British persiflage. Signs of grim envy did not spoil the joke, for there were those of as grim a magnanimity behind it all; and the pale lad himself, taking their nonsense in the best of part, yet shyly, as though they had a right to complain, and he only wished they could all have been wounded and sent home together, was their match in simple subtlety and hidden kindness. And between them all they were better worth seeing and hearing than the moonlight and the guns.

It is easy to make too much of a trifle that was not one to me, but in a sense my first casualty, almost a poignant experience. But there are no trifles in the trenches in the dead of winter; there is not enough happening; everything that does happen is magnified accordingly; and the one man hit on a quiet day is a greater celebrity than the last survivor of his platoon in the day of big things. The one man gets an audience, and the audience has time to think twice about him.

In the same way nothing casts a heavier gloom than an isolated death in action, such as the one which had occurred here only the previous day. All ranks were still talking about the man who had lain unburied where his comrades were now laughing in the moonlight; detail upon detail I heard before the night was out, and all had the pathos of the isolated case, the vividness of a portrait as against a group. The man had been a Lewis gunner, and he had died flushed with the crowning success of his career. That was the consoling detail: in his last week on earth, in full view of friend and foe, he had brought off the kind of shot a whole battalion boasts about. His bird still lay on No-Man's Land, a jumble of wire and mangled planes; not the sight to sober a successful sportsman, and him further elated by the promise of special and immediate leave. No time for a lad of his mettle to weary of well-doing; and he knew of a sniper worth adding to his bag. The sniper, however, would seem to have known of him, and in the ensuing duel took special care of himself. Not so the swollen-hearted sportsman who was going on leave and meant earning it. Many shots had been exchanged without result; at last, unable to bear it any longer, our poor man had leapt upon the parapet, only to drop back like a stone, shot dead not by the other duellist but by a second sniper posted elsewhere for the purpose. And this tragically ordinary tragedy was all the talk that night over the mugs. Grim snatches linger. One quite sorrowful chum regretted the other's braces, buried with him and of all things the most useless in a grave, and he himself in need of a new pair. It did seem as though he might have taken them off the body, and with the flown spirit's hearty sanction.

They did not say where they had buried him, but our sunken roadside was not without its own wooden cross of older standing. It was the tiniest and flimsiest I ever saw, and yet it had stood through other days, when the road was in other hands; those other hands must have put it up. 'An Unknown British Hero of the R.F.A.' was all the legend they had left to endure with this ironical tenacity.

About midnight we came to an end of our water, supplied each morning by a working-party detailed for the job: with more water we might have done worse than keep open all night and kill the bitter day with sleep. As it was, we were soon creeping through a man-hole curtained by a frozen blanket into the corrugated core of the sand-bagged gunyah. It was as much as elbow-high down the middle of the span; the beds were side by side, so close together that we had to get in by the foot; and only for a wager would I have attempted to undress in the space remaining.

But not for any money on such a night! A particularly feeble oil-stove, but all we had to warm the hut by day, had been doing what it could for us here at the eleventh hour; but all it had done was to stud the roof with beads of moisture and draw the damp out of the blankets. We got between them in everything except our boots; even trench-coats were not discarded, nor fleece linings any longer to be despised. The other man was soon asleep. But I had provided myself with appropriate reading, and for some time burnt a candle to old James Grant and The Romance of War.

There are those who delight in declaring there is no romance in this war; there was enough for me that night. Not many inches from my side the nearest shell had burst, not many days ago by some miracle without blowing in a sand-bag; not many inches from my head, and perhaps no deeper in the earth, lay the skull of our 'unknown hero of the R.F.A.' I for one did not sleep the worse for his honoured company, or for our common lullaby the guns.

AN INTERRUPTED LUNCH

But there was another side to our life up the line, thanks to the regal hospitality of Battalion Headquarters. Thither we were bidden to all meals, and there we presented ourselves with feverish punctuality at least three times a day.

It was only about a minute's walk along the trench, past more dug-outs lit by cigarette-ends, past a trench store-cupboard quietly labelled BOMBS, and a sentry in a sand-bagged cul-de-sac. The door at which we knocked was no more imposing than our own, the sanctuary within no roomier, but like the deck-house of a well-appointed yacht after a tramp's forecastle. Art-green walls and fixed settees, a narrow table all spotless napery and sparkling glass, forks and spoons as brilliant as a wedding-present, all these were there or I have dreamt them. I would even swear to flowers on the table, if it were a case of swearing one way or other. But what they gave us to eat, with two exceptions, I cannot in the least remember; it was immaterial in that atmosphere and company, though I recall the other man's bated breathings on the point. My two exceptions were porridge at breakfast and scones at tea; both were as authentic as the mess-waiter's speech; and it would not have surprised me if the porridge had been followed by trout from the burn, so much was that part of the Line just then a part of Scotland.

It was a genial atmosphere in more ways than one. Always on coming in one's spectacles turned to ground-glass and one's out-door harness to melting lead. The heat came up an open stairway from the bowels of the earth, as did the chimney which I painfully mistook for a hand-rail the first night, when the Colonel was kind enough to take me down below. It was the first deep dug-out I had seen in working order, and it seemed to me deliciously safe and snug; the officers' berths in fascinating tiers, again as on shipboard, all but the Colonel's own, by itself at one end. It made me very jealous, yet rather proud, when I thought of our freezing lair upon the sunken road.

Then, before we went, he took me up to an O.P. on top of all. I think we climbed up to it out of the cul-de-sac, and I know I cowered behind a chunk of parapet; but what I remember best is the zig-zag labyrinth in the foreground, that unending open grave with upturned earth complete, yet quiet as any that ever was filled in; and then the wide sweep of moonlit snow, enemy country nearly all, but at the moment still and peaceful as an arctic floe. Our own trenches the only solid signs of war, like the properties in front of a panorama; not a shot or a sound to give the rest more substance than a painted back-cloth. It was one of those dead pauses that occur on all but the noisiest nights, and make the whole war nowhere more unreal than on the battle-field.

But when the very next day was at its quietest we had just the opposite experience. We were sitting at luncheon in this friendly mess, and the guns might have been a thousand miles away until they struck up all at once, like a musical-box in the middle of a tune. Their guns, this time; but you would not have thought it from the faces round the table. One or two exchanged glances; a lifted eyebrow was answered by a smile; but the conversation went on just the same until the officer nearest the door withdrew detachedly. New subject no longer avoidable, but treated with becoming levity. Not a bombardment, just a Strafe, we gathered; it might have been with blank shell, had we not heard them bursting. Exit another officer; enter man from below. Something like telegram in his hand: retaliation requested by front line. 'Put it through to Brigade.' Further retirements from board; less noise for moment. New sound: enemy 'plane over us, seeing what they've done. New row next door: our machine-guns on enemy 'plane! New note in distance: retaliation to esteemed order.... Other man and I alone at table, dying to go out and see fun, but obviously not our place. And then in a minute it is all over, not quite as quickly as it began, but getting on that way. Strafe stopped: 'plane buzzing away again: machine-guns giving it up as a bad job: cheery return of Belisarii, in the order of their going, Colonel last and cheeriest of all.

'Had my hair parted by a whizz-bang,' says he, 'up in that O.P. we were in last night.'

And, as he replenished a modest cup, the curtain might have fallen on the only line I remember in the whole impromptu piece, which could not have played quicker as a music-hall sketch, or held a packed audience more entranced than the two civilian supers who had the luck to be on the stage.

But we had to pay for our entertainment; for although it turned out to have been an absolutely bloodless Strafe, yet a portion of our parapet had been blown in, which made it inexpedient for us to go round the front line that afternoon, as previously arranged by our indulgent hosts. In the evening they were going into reserve, and another famous Regiment coming to 'take over.' The new-comers, however, were just as good to us in their turn; and the new Colonel so kind as to take me round himself on Christmas morning.

CHRISTMAS DAY

The tiny hut is an abode of darkness made visible by a single candle, mounted in its own grease in the worst available position for giving light, lest the opening of the door cast the faintest beam into the sunken road outside. On the shelf flush with the door glimmer parental urns with a large family of condensed-milk tins, opened and unopened, full and empty; packing-cases in similar stages litter the duck-board flooring, or pile it wall-high in the background; trench-coats, gas-masks, haversacks and helmets hang from nails or repose on a ledge of the inner wall, which is sunken roadside naked and unashamed. Two weary figures cower over the boiler fire; they are the other man and yet another who has come up for the night. A third person, who may look more like me than I feel like him, hovers behind them, smoking and peering at his watch. It is the last few minutes of Christmas Eve, and for a long hour there has been little or nothing doing. Earlier in the evening, from seven or so onwards, there seemed no end to the queue of armed men, calling for their mug of cocoa and their packet of biscuits, either singly, each for himself, or with dixies and sand-bags to be filled for comrades on duty in the trenches.

The quiet has been broken only by the sibilant song of the boiler, by desultory conversation and bursts of gunfire as spasmodic and inconsequent. Often a machine-gun has beaten a brief but furious tattoo on the doors of darkness; but now come clogged and ponderous footfalls—mud to mud on the duck-boards leading from the communication trench—and a chit is handed in from the outer moonlight.

'24—12—17.

'To Y.M.C.A. Canteen, '— Avenue.

'DEAR SIRS,—I will be much obliged if you will supply the bearer with hot cocoa (sufficient for 90 men) which I understand you are good enough to issue to units in this line. The party are taking 2 hot-food containers for the purpose.

'Thanking you in anticipation, 'I am, yours faithfully, '(Illegible), 'O/C B Co., '1/8 (Undesirable).'

Torpid trio are busy men once more. Not enough cocoa ready-made for ninety; fresh brew under way in fewer seconds than it takes to state the fact. Third person already anchored beside open packing-case, enormous sand-bag gaping between his knees, little sealed packets flying through his hands from box to bag in twins and triplets. By now it is Christmas morning; cakes and cigarettes are forthwith added to statutory biscuits, and a sack is what is wanted. Third person makes shift with second sand-bag, which having filled, he leaves his colleagues working like benevolent fiends in the steam of fragrant cauldrons, and joins the group outside among the shell-holes.

They are consuming interim dividends of the nightly fare, as they stand about in steely silhouette against the shrouded moonlight. The scene is not quite so picturesque as it was last night, when no star of heaven could live in the light of the frosty moon and every helmet was a shining halo; to-night the only twinkle to be seen is under a helmet's rim.

'Merry Christmas, sir, an' many of 'em,' says a Tyneside voice, getting in the first shot of a severe bombardment. The third person retaliates with appropriate spirit; the interchange could not have been franker or heartier in the days of actual peace on earth and apparent good-will among men. But here they both are for a little space this Christmas morning. Cannon may drum it in with thunderous irony, and some corner-man behind a machine-gun oblige with what sounds exactly like a solo on the bones, but here in the midst of those familiar alarms the Spirit of Christmas is abroad on the battle-field. He may be frightened away—or become a casualty—at any moment. One lucky flourish with the bones, one more addition to these sharp-edged shell-holes, and how many of the party would have a groan left in him? One of them groans in spirit as he thinks, never so vividly, of countless groups as full of gay vitality as this one, blown out of existence in a blinding flash. But his hardy friends are above such morbid imaginings; the cold appears to be their only trouble, and of it they make light enough as they stamp their feet. Some are sea-booted in sand-bags, and what with their jerkins and low, round helmets, look more like a watch in oilskins and sou'-westers than a party of Infantry.

'We nevaw died o' wintaw yet,' says the Tynesider. 'It takes a lot to kill an old soljaw.' But he owns he was a shipyard hand before the war; and not one of them was in the Army.

All hope it is the last Christmas of the war, but the Tyneside prognostication of 'anothaw ten yeaws' is received with perfect equanimity. There is general agreement, too, when the same oracle dismisses the latest peace offer as 'blooff.' But it must be confessed that articulate ardour is slightly damped until somebody starts a subject a great deal nearer home.

'Who'd have thought that we should live to see a Y.M. in the support line!'

Flattering echoes from entire group.

'Do you remember that chap who kept us all awake in barracks, talking of it?'

'I nevaw believed him. I thought it was a myth, sir. And nothing to pay an' all! It must be costing the Y.M. a canny bit o' money, sir?'

The third person—who has been hovering on the verge of the inveterate first—only commits himself to the statement that he helped to give away 785 cups of cocoa and packets of biscuits the night before. Rapid calculations ensue. 'Why, that must be nearly ten pounds a night, sir?'

'Something like that.'

'Heaw that, Corporal! An' now it's cigarettes an' cakes an' all!'

But the containers are ready, lids screwed down upon their steaming contents. Strong arms hoist them upon stronger backs; the plethoric sand-bags are shouldered with still less ado, and off go the party into the slate-coloured night, off through the communication trenches into the firing-line they are to hold for England until the twelve hundred and thirty-ninth daybreak of the war.

Peering after them with wistful glasses, the third person relapses altogether into the first. Take away the odd two hundred, and for a thousand days and nights my heart has been where their muffled feet will be treading in another minute. Yes; a round thousand must be almost the exact length of days since I first came out here in the spirit, and to stay. But never till this year did I seriously dream of following in the flesh, or till this moment feel the front line like a ball at my feet. Even the day before yesterday the arrangement was not so definite as it is to-day; it was not the Colonel himself who was to have taken us round by special favour and appointment. Yet how easily, had the Strafe happened half-an-hour later than it did, might we not have come in for it, perhaps at the very place where the parapet was blown down! It would have been a wonderful experience, especially as there were no casualties. Will anything of the kind happen to-day? I have a feeling that something may; but then I have had that feeling every sentient moment up the Line. And nothing that can come can come amiss; that is another of my feelings here, if not the strongest of them all. This Christmas morning it rings almost like a carol in the heart, almost like a peal of Christmas bells—jangled indeed by the heart's own bitter flaws, and yet piercing sweet as Life itself.

But for all my elderly civilian excitement, before a risk too tiny to enter a young fighting head at all, sleep does not fail me on a new couch of my own construction. The sand-bagged lair was none too dry in the late hard frost; in the unseasonable thaw that seems to be setting in, it is no place for crabbed age. Youth is welcome to the two beds with the water now standing on their indiarubber sheets, and youth seems quite honestly to prefer them; so I make mine on the biscuit-boxes in the shed, turn my toes to the still glowing coke in the boiler fire, press my soles to the hot-water bottle which has distinguished itself by freezing during the day, and huddle down as usual in all the indoor and outdoor garments I have with me, under my share of the blankets, which I have been drying assiduously every evening. The Romance of War performs its nightly unromantic office ... and I have had many a worse night upon a spring-mattress.

Colonel finished breakfast when I reach the mess; ready for me by the time I have had mine. We glove and muffle ourselves, adjust gas-masks 'at the ready,' and sally forth on his common round and my high adventure, tapping the still slippery duck-boards with our sticks.

A colourless morning, neither freezing nor thawing; visibility probably low, luminosity certainly mediocre; in fact, typical Christmas weather of the modern realistic school, as against the Christmas Number weather of the last ten days. Yet it is the Christmas Number atmosphere that haunts me as an aura the more tenacious for its utter absence on all sides: the sprig of holly in the cake, the presents on the table, the joys of parent and child—never more at one—and blinding visions in both capacities, down to that last war-time Christmas dinner at the Carlton ... such are the sights that await me after all in the front-line trench! I have dreamt of it for years, yet now that I am here it is of the dead years I dream, or of this Christmas morning anywhere but where it is one's beatitude to be spending it.

Not that I fail to see a good deal of what is before my eyes at last; but never for many yards is the trench that we are in the only one I seem to see, and a comparison between the two is irresistible. Perhaps the width and solidity of this trench would impress me less if it were not all so different from Belgium as I all but knew it in 1915; the machine-gunners at their posts in the deep bays, like shepherds sheltering behind a wall, yet somehow able to see through the wall, would stand out less if the fire-step also were manned in the old way. But now trenches are held more by machinery and by fewer men, at any rate, in daytime; and at night men evidently do not sleep so near their work as then they did; at least, I look in vain for dug-outs in this sector of the front line. And I still look in vain for trouble, though all the time I feel all sorts of possibilities impending: a strange mixture of curiosity and dread it is—ardent curiosity, and quite pleasurable dread—that weaves itself into the warp of all inward and outward impressions whatsoever: can it be peculiar to self-ridden civilians, or are there really brave men like the Colonel in front of me (with a bar to his D.S.O.) who have undergone similar sensations at their baptism of fire?

It is not exactly mine; nothing comes anything like so near me as that sniper's bullet on the way up the other day; but little black bursts do keep occurring high overhead, where one of our airmen is playing peep among the clouds. The fragments must be falling somewhere in the neighbourhood; and a more alarming kind of shell has just burst on the high ground between our parados and the support line. Not very close—I must have been listening to something else—but the Colonel points out the smoking place with his stick and his quiet smile. His smile is part of him, very quiet and contained, full of easy-going power, and a kindness incapable of condescension. He might be my country-house host pointing out the excellence of his crop, but his touch is lighter and I am not expected to admire. He is, of all soldiers I ever met, just the one I would choose to be alongside if I had to be hit. I don't believe his face would alter very much, and I should be dying not to alter it more than I could help.

But, in spite of all interior preparation, it is not to be. He has given me a glimpse of No-Man's Land, not through a periscope but in a piece of ordinary looking-glass; we are nearing the damaged place where his presence is required and mine emphatically is not. Not that he says anything of the sort, but I see it in his kindly smile as he hands me over to his runner for safe-conduct to the place from whence I came. Still as much disappointed as relieved, as though a definite excitement had been denied to me, I turned and went with equal reluctance and alacrity.

'The bravest officer in the British Army!' was the runner's testimony to our friend. I have heard the honest words before, but this hero-worshipper had chapter and verse for his creed: 'Six times he has been wounded in this war, and never yet gone back to Blighty for a wound!'

I had not noticed the six gold stripes—if any—but it is not everybody who wears his full allowance. And if ever I met a man who cared less than most brave men about all such things, I believe I said good-bye to him last Christmas Day.

We were to meet again in the evening; in the meantime I was to have my Christmas dinner with the other Colonel and his merry men, now in reserve. I found them in an ex-Hun dug-out, more like a forecastle than the other headquarters; everything underground, and the bunks ranged round the board; but there was the same sheen on the table-cloth, the same glitter of glass and plate, the same good cheer and a turkey worthy of the day, and a ham worthy of the turkey, and a plum-pudding worthy of them both. It is not for the guest of a mess to say grace in public; but Christmas dinner in the trenches is a case apart. As the school tag might have had it, non cuivis civi talia contingunt.

There were crackers, too, I suddenly remember, and the old idiotic paper caps and mottoes, and Christmas cards wherever one went. In the new legions there is nearly always some cunning hand to supply the unit with a topical Christmas card: one of our two Battalions had a beauty, and even the Y.M.C.A. made bold to circulate an artistic apotheosis of our quarters on the sunken road. But those are not the Christmas cards I still preserve; my ill-gotten souvenirs are typewritten scraps on typewriting-paper, unillustrated, but all the more to the point: 'Best wishes for Xmas and Good Luck in 1918, from the Brigadier and Staff, —th Infantry Brigade.'—'Christmas Greetings and All Good Luck from —th Infantry Brigade Headquarters.'—'Christmas Greetings and Good Luck from —th Divisional Artillery.' I must say this kind appealed to me, though I sent away a good many of the more ambitious variety. In neither was there any conventional nonsense about a 'happy' or even a 'merry' Christmas; and that, in view of the well-known perversity of the Comic Spirit, may have been one reason why so much merriment accrued. Nor did the contrast between unswerving ceremonial and a sardonic simplicity, as shown in this matter of the Christmas cards, begin or end there; for while I had followed crystal and fine table-linen into reserve for my Christmas dinner, the hospitable board behind the front line was now spread with newspapers, and we drank both our whisky-and-soda and our coffee out of the same enamelled cup.

The Colonel who had taken me into the front line after breakfast was not at dinner that night; for all his wounds he had gone down with common influenza, and I was desolated. It was my last chance of thanking him, as the other man and I were leaving in the early morning. All day I had been thinking of all that I had seen, and of all I had but foreseen, though so vividly that I felt more and more as though I had actually had some definite escape; besides, the things I had heard about him after we parted made me covet the honour of shaking hands once more with so very brave a man. I had my wish. In the middle of dinner a servant emerged from below to say: 'The Colonel would like to see the Y.M.C.A. officer before he went.'

I can see him still, as I found him, hot and coughing on the bunk in the corner by itself. 'I thought you would be interested to hear,' said he, 'that the very minute you left me this morning a rum-jar burst on the parados just behind me. You know how I wear my helmet, with the strap behind? It blew it off.'

So my escape had been fairly definite after all, and the thing I was so ready for had really happened 'the very minute' my back was turned! But that, unhappily, is not the whole coincidence. Five months later it was written of 'this good and gallant leader' that 'while inspecting his battalion in the trenches he was struck by a fragment of shell from a trench mortar (i.e. a rum-jar) and killed instantaneously.' My parenthesis; the rest from The Times notice, which also bears out the story of the six wounds, except that they were seven, and four of them earned ('with an immediate award of the D.S.O.') on a single occasion. There is more in the notice that I should like to quote, more still that I could say even on the strength of that one morning's work; but who am I to praise so grand a man? I only know that I shall never see another Christmas without seeing that front-line trench, and a quiet, dark man in the pride and prime of perfect soldierhood, self-saddled with an old camp-follower who felt as a child beside him.

THE BABES IN THE TRENCHES

In the morning we made our tracks in virgin snow. It had fallen heavily in the night, and was still falling as we turned into the trench. So was a light shower of shell; but it blew over; and now our good luck seemed almost certain to attend us to our journey's end.

The snow thinned off as we plodded on our way. But it had altered and improved the trenches out of knowledge, lying thick along the top on either hand and often half-way down the side, so that we seemed like Gullivers striding between two chains of Lilliputian Alps. It was nevertheless hard going in our valley, where the duck-boards were snowed under for long stretches without a break, and warmer work in my fleece lining than I had known it yet. My gas-mask was like a real mill-stone round the neck; and though the other man had possessed himself of part of my impedimenta, that only made me feel my age the more acutely. Almost a great age I felt that morning; for nights on packing-cases in a low temperature, and an early start on biscuits and condensed-milk prepared with cold water, after short commons of sleep, are the kind of combination that will find a man out. I was not indeed complaining, but neither was I as observant as I might have been. I had been over this part of the ground by myself the day before, on the way to my Christmas dinner. It did look rather different in the snow, but that was to be expected, and the other man knew the way well. So I understood, and he emphatically affirmed the supposition on such provocation as I from time to time felt justified in giving the voluntary bearer of my pack. It was only when we came to some suspiciously unfamiliar landmark, something important (but I honestly forget what) in a bay by itself, that I asserted myself sufficiently to call a halt.

'We never passed that before!'

'Oh, yes, we did. I'm sure we did. I think I remember it.'

That ought not to have satisfied me; but you cannot openly discredit a man who insists on carrying your pack. I was too fatigued to take it from him, and not competent to take the lead. On he led me, perspiring my misgivings at every pore; but under a tangled bridge of barbed wire I made a firmer stand.

'Anyhow, you don't remember this!' I asserted point-blank.

'No. I can't say I do.'

'Then how do you account for it?'

'It must have been put up in the night.'

I cannot remember by what further resource of casuistry that young man induced me to follow him another yard; yet so it was, and all the shame be mine. He himself was the next to falter and stand still in his tracks, and finally to face me with a question whose effrontery I can still admire:

'What would you do if we met a Hun? Put your hands up?'

We were, in fact, once more impinging upon the firing line, and by a trench at the time, apparently, not much in use. I know it seemed long hours since we had encountered a soul; but then it might have been for the best part of another hour that my guilty guide now left me in order to ascertain the worst, and I do not seriously suppose it was very many minutes. I remember cooling off against the side of the trench, and hearing absolutely nothing all the time. That I still think remarkable. It was not snowing; the sun shone; visibility must have been better than for two whole days; and yet nothing was happening. I might have been waiting in some Highland glen, or in a quarry in the wilds of Dartmoor. I think that particular silence was as impressive, as intimidating, as the very heaviest firing that I heard in all my four months at the front.

No harm came of our misadventure; it was possibly less egregious than it sounds. A wrong turning in the snow had taken us perhaps a mile out of our way; but a trench mile is a terribly long one, and I know how much I should like to add for the state of the duck-boards on this occasion, and how much more for that of a lame old duck who thought they were never, never coming to an end! The valley of the guns was nothing after them, though the guns were active at the time, an anti-aircraft battery taking an academic interest in a humming speck on high. Beyond the valley ran the road, and beyond the road the river, where we were to have caught a boat. Of course we had just succeeded in missing it. A homeward-bound lorry picked us up at last. And we were in plenty of time for the plain mid-day meal at our humble headquarters in the town. But by then I was done to the world and dead to shame. I suppose I have led too soft a life, taking very little exercise for its own sake, though occasionally going to the other extreme from an ulterior motive. So I have been deservedly tired once or twice in my time; but I didn't know what it was to be done up before last Boxing Day.

The short mile down to the hut that afternoon was the longest and worst of all. Stiffness was setting in, and the snow so deep in the ruinous streets; but every yard of the way I looked forward to my sheetless bed; and few things in life have disappointed me so little. The fire was out, it seemed, and was worth lighting first. There was a sensuous joy about that last purely voluntary effort and delay. I even think I waited to let my old hot-water bottle share in the triumphal entry between blankets that were at least dry, plentiful, and soft as a feather-bed after the lids of those packing-cases up the Line!

And it was our Christmas concert in the hut that evening: the copious entertainment disturbed without spoiling my rest, rather bringing it home to every aching inch of me as the heavenly thing it was. Song and laughter travelled up the hut, and filtered through to me refined and rarefied by far more than the little distance. Somebody came in and made tea. It was better than being ill. I lay there till nine next morning; then went down to the Officers' Baths, and came out feeling younger than at any period of actual but insensate youth.

DETAILS

ORDERLY MEN

He who loves a good novel will find himself in clover in a Y.M.C.A. hut at the front. Not that he will have much time to read one there, except as I read my night-cap The Romance of War; but a better book of the same name will never stop writing itself out before his eyes, a book all dialogue and illustrations, yet chock-full of marvellous characters, drawn to a man without a word of commentary or analysis. To a man, advisedly, since it will be a novel without a heroine; on the other hand, all the men and boys will be heroes, at any rate to the kind of reader I have in mind. Something will depend on him; he will have to apply himself, as much as to any other kind of reading. He must have eyes to see, brains to translate, a heart to love or pity or admire. He must have the power to penetrate under other skins, to tremble for them more than for his own, to glow and sweat with them, to shiver in shoes he is not fit to wear. Many can go as far for people who never existed outside some author's brain; these are they on whom the most stupendous of unwritten romances is least likely to be lost. It lies open to all who care to take their stand behind a hut counter in a forward area in France.

The character to be seen there, and to be loved at sight! The adventures to be heard at first-hand, and sometimes even shared! The fun, the pathos, the underlying horror, but the grandeur lying deeper yet, all to be encountered together at any minute of any working hour! The Romance of War it is, but not only the romance; and talking of my sedative, with all affection for an author who once kept me only too wide awake, it was not of him that I thought by day behind my counter. It was of Dickens. It was of Hugo. It was of Reade, who might have done the best battle in British fiction (and did one of the very best sea-fights), of Scott and Stevenson and the one or two living fathers of families who will die as hard as theirs. Their children were always coming to life before our eyes, especially the Dickens progeny. Sapper Pinch was a friend of mine, with one or two near relations in the R.A.M.C. There were several Private Tapleys, and not one of them a bore; on the contrary, they were worth their weight in gold. And there was an older man whose real name was obviously Sikes, though the worst thing we knew about him was that he smoked an ounce of Nosegay every day he was down, and never said please or thank-you. Once, when we had not seen him for sixteen days, he knew there was something else he wanted but could not remember what. 'Nosegays!' I could tell him, and planked a packet on the counter. It was the one time I saw him smile.

But it was not only business hours that brought forth these immortals; two of the best were always with us in the superbly contrasted persons of our two orderlies. The slower and clumsier of the pair was by rights an Oxfordshire shepherd; in the Army, even under necessity's sternest law, he was matter in the wrong place altogether. Oxfordshire may not be actually a part of Wessex, but there is one part of Oxfordshire as remote as the scene of any of the Wessex Novels, and that was our Strephon's native place. He might have been the real and original Gabriel Oak—as Mr. Hardy found him, not as we fortunately know the bucolic hero of Far from the Madding Crowd.

Our Gabriel was the simplest bumpkin ever seen or heard off the London stage. He it was who, in his early days in France, had heavily inquired: 'Who be this 'ere Fritz they be arl tarkin' about?' Thus did he habitually conjugate the verb to be; but all his locutions and most of his manners and customs, his puzzled head-scratchings, his audible self-communings, his crass sagacity and his simple cunning, were pastoral conventions of quite time-honoured theatricality. His very walk, for all his drills, was the ponderous waddle of the stage rustic. But on his own showing he had (like another Tommy) 'proved one too many for his teachers' at an early stage of his military education. Not all their precept and profanity, not all his pristine ardour as a volunteer, had sufficed to put poor Gabriel on terms of adequate familiarity with his rifle.

'I couldn' make nothin' of it, sir,' he would say with rueful candour. 'So they couldn' make nothin' o' me.'

His simplicity was a joy, though he was sometimes simple to a fault. One morning I caught him draining our tea-pot as a loving-cup: matted head thrown back, brawny elbows lifted, and the spout engulfed in his honest maw: a perfect silhouette, not to be destroyed by a sound, much less a word of protest, even had we not been devoted to our gentle savage. But one of us did surreptitiously attend to the spout before tea-time. And once before my eyes his ready lips sucked the condensed-milk off our tin-opener before plunging it into a tin of potted meat. He had a moustache of obsolete luxuriance, I remember with a shudder in this connection; but the last time I saw him the moustache was not.

'You see, sir,' explained Gabriel, regretfully, 'I had a cold, an' it arl ...'

I hope my muscles were still under due control. To know our Gabriel was to perish rather than hurt his feelings; for he had the softest heart of his own, and in Oxfordshire a wife and children to share its affections with his ewes and lambs. 'An' I think a lot on 'em, too, sir,' said Gabriel, when he showed me the full family group (self in uniform) done on his last 'leaf.' Really a sweet simpleton, even when (as I was nearly forgetting) he announced a brand-new Brigadier-General, who had honoured me with a visit, as 'A gen'leman to see you, sir!'

The only man of us who had the heart to tell the angelic Gabriel off was his brother orderly, a respectable and patriotic Huish, if such a combination can be conceived. Our Mr. Huish was the gentleman who always said it wanted five minutes to the 'alf-hour when it wanted at least ten, and too often sped the last of our lingering guests with insult into outer darkness. Like his prototype he was a fiery little Londoner, with a hacking cough and a husky voice ever rising to a shout in his dealings with bovine Gabriel. There was nothing of the beasts of the field about our Huish; he was the terrier type, and more than true to it in his fidelity to his temporary masters. At us he never snarled. His special province was the boiler stove; he was generally blacked up to the red rims of his eyes, like a seaside minstrel, and might have been collecting money in his banjo as we saw him first of a dim morning. But the instrument was only our frying-pan carried at arm's length, and our approval of an unconscionable lot of rashers all the recognition he required. 'W'en I 'as plenty I likes to give plenty,' was his disreputable watchword in these matters. I am afraid he was not supposed to cook for us at all.

Huish was always bustling, or at least shambling with alacrity; whereas Gabriel went about his lightest business with ponderous deliberation and puzzled frown. Both were men of forty who had done the right thing early in the war; they had nothing else in common except the inglorious job which they owed to their respective infirmities. Huish, after many rejections on the score of his, had yet contrived to land in khaki at Le Havre on the last day of the first battle of Ypres; and though he had never been nearer the fighting than he was with us, no one who knew his story or himself could have grudged him his 1914 ribbon. His canine delight, on learning that he was just entitled to it, was a thing to see and to enter into.

Let us hope Gabriel did; he was not very charitable about Huish behind his back. It was Gabriel's boast that he had 'never been in the 'ands of the police,' and his shame to inform us that Huish had. But the sun has its spots, and the overwhelming superiority of Huish in munitions of altercation was perhaps some excuse. Daily we caught his rising voice and Gabriel's rumbling monotone; what it was about we never knew; but Huish had all the nerves in the kitchen, and the shepherd must have been a heavyweight on them at times. Their language, however, as we heard it under mutual provocation, was either a considerable compliment to the Y.M.C.A. or an exclusive credit to themselves. Gabriel was duly archangelic in this regard; the other's only freedom a habit of calling a thing an 'ell of a thing, and on occasion an Elizabethan expressiveness, entirely inoffensive in his mouth.

I wanted their photographs to take with me when I left, and had prevailed upon them to get taken together at my expense. The result lies before me as I write. Both are washed, brushed up, shaven and uniformed out of daily knowledge. Huish stands keenly at attention, as smart as he could make himself; it is not his fault that the sleeves of his new tunic come down nearly to his finger-tips. On his right shoulder rests the forgiving paw of Gabriel; a perceptibly sardonic accentuation of the crow's-feet round his eyes may perhaps be attributed to this prompting of the shepherd's heart or the photographer's finesse. But the pose was a consummation; it was in the course of a preliminary transaction that their excessive gratification obliged me to disclaim benevolence.

'I shall want some of the copies for myself, you know,' I had warned them both.

'Quite right, sir!' cried Huish, heartily. 'It's like a man with a dog an' a bitch—'e must 'ave 'is pick o' the pups!'

Huish could take the counter at a pinch, but it was neither his business nor his pleasure; and our gentle shepherd found French coinage as dark a mystery as the British rifle. But we were very often assisted by an unpaid volunteer, another great character in his way. We never knew his name, and to me at least he was a new type. A Hull lad, eighteen years old, private in a Labour Battalion employed near the town, he must have had work enough by day and night to satisfy even one of his strength and build, which were those of a little gorilla. And yet never a free evening had this boy but he must spend it behind our counter, slaving like the best of us for sheer love. But it was the work he loved; he was a little shop-keeper born and bred; his heart was in the till at home; that was what brought him hot-foot to ours; and his passionate delight in the mere routine of retail trade was the new thing to me in human boyhood.

At first I had wondered, the hobby seemed so unnatural: at first I even kept an eye on him and on the till. Our leader had gone on leave before the New Year; nobody seemed to know how far he had encouraged the boy, or the origin of his anomalous footing in the hut; and we were taking a cool thousand francs a day. But our young volunteer bore microscopic scrutiny, but repaid it all. His was not only a labour of love unashamed, but the joyous exercise of a gift, the triumphant display of an inherent power. He beat the best of us behind a counter. It was his element, not ours for all the will and skill in the world; he was a fish among swimmers, a professional among amateurs, and the greatest disciplinarian of us all. The home till may have been behind a bar in the worst part of Hull, long practice in prompt refusal have given him his short way with old soldiers opening negotiations out of their turn. It was a good way, however, as cheery as it was firm. I can hear it now:

'Naw, yer dawn't, Jock! Get away back an' coom oop in't queue like oother people!'

It was never resented. Though not even one of us, but the youngest and lowliest of themselves, that urchin by his own virtue exercised the authority of a truculent N.C.O. with the whole military machine behind him. I never heard a murmur against him, or witnessed the least reluctance to obey his ruling. And with equal impunity he addressed all alike as 'Jock.'

But that, though one of his many and quaint idiosyncrasies, was perhaps the covert compliment that took the edge off all the rest.

And it brings me to the Jocks themselves, who deserve a place apart from Y.M.C.A. orderlies and the best of boys in a Labour Battalion.

THE JOCKS

First a word about this generic term of 'Jock.' I use it advisedly, yet not without a qualm. It is not for a civilian to drop into military familiarities on the strength of a winter with the Expeditionary Force; but this sobriquet has spread beyond all Army areas; like 'Tommy,' but with a difference worth considering, it has passed into the language of the man still left in the street. If not, it will; for you have only to see him at his job in the war, doing it in a way and a spirit all his own, and a Jock is a Jock to you ever after. As the cricketer said about the yorker, what else can you call him?

The first time the word slipped off my tongue, except behind their backs, and I found I had called a superb young Seaforth Highlander 'Jock' to his noble face, I stood abashed before him. It sounded an unpardonable liberty; apologise I must, and did.

'It's a name I am proud to be called by,' said he quite simply. I never committed the apology again.

It was not as though one had called an English soldier 'Tommy' to his face; the Jock's answer brought that home to me, and with something like a shock—not because 'Jock' was evidently rather more than a term of endearment, but because 'Tommy' suddenly seemed rather less. Each carried its own nuance, its quite separate implication, and somehow the later term took higher ground. I wondered how much later it was. Did it begin in South Africa? There were no Jocks in Barrack-Room Ballads; but there was 'Tommy,' the poem; and between those immortal lines I read my explanation. It was from them I had learnt, long years before either war, that it was actually possible for purblind peace-lovers to look down upon the British soldier, under the name those lines dinned in. The Jocks had not been christened in those dead days; that was their luck; that was the difference. Their name belonged to the spacious times which have given the fighting-man the place of honour in all true hearts.

Hard on Tommy! As for the Jocks, they have earned their good name if men ever did; but I am to speak of them only as I saw them across a Y.M.C.A. counter, demanding 'twust' without waste of syllables, or 'wrichting-pads,' or 'caun'les'; huge men with little voices, little men with enormous muscles; men of whalebone with the quaint, stiff gait engendered by the kilt, looking as though their upper halves were in strait waistcoats, simply because the rest of them goes so free; figures of droll imperturbability, of bold and handsome sang-froid, hunting in couples among the ruins for any fun or trouble that might be going. 'As if the town belonged to them!' said one who loved the sight of them; but I always thought the distinctive thing about the Jock was his air of belonging to the town, ruined or otherwise, or to the bleak stretch of war-eaten countryside where one had the good fortune to encounter him. His matter-of-fact stolidity, his dry scorn of discomfort, the soul above hardship looking out of his keen yet dreamy eyes, the tight smile on his proud, uncomplaining lips—to meet all these in a trench was to feel the trench transformed to some indestructible stone alley of the Old Town. These men might have been born and bred in dug-outs, and played all their lives in No-Man's Land, as town children play about a street and revel in its dangers.

I am proud to remember that they held the part of the line I was in at Christmas. I saw them do everything but fight, and that I had no wish to see as a spectator; but everybody knows how they set about it, the enemy best of all. I have seen them, however, pretty soon after a raid: it was like talking to a man who had just made a hundred at Lord's: our hut was the Pavilion. I never saw them with their blood up, and to see them merely under fire is to see them just themselves—not even abnormally normal like less steady souls.

Said a Black Watchman in the hearing of a friend of mine, as he mended a parapet under heavy fire, in the worst days of '15: 'I wish they'd stop their bloody sniping—and let me get on with my work!'

The Jock all over! So a busy man swears at a wasp; the Jock at war is just a busy man until something happens to put a stop to his business. In the meantime he is not complaining; he is not asking you when this dreadful war will finish; he is not telling you it can never be finished by fighting. He went to the war as a bridegroom to his bride, and he has the sense and virtue to make the best of his bargain till death or peace doth them part. He may sigh for his release like other poor devils; his pride will not let him sigh audibly; and as for 'getting out of it,' divorce itself is not more alien to his stern spirit. It is true that he has the business in his blood: not the Covenanters only but the followers of Montrose and Claverhouse were Jocks before him. It is also true that even he is not always at concert pitch; but his nerves do not relax or snap in damp or cold, as may the nerves of a race less inured through the centuries to hardship and the incidence of war. In bitter fighting there is nothing to choose between the various branches of the parent oak. The same sound sap runs through them all. But in bitter weather on the Western Front give me a hutful of Jocks! If only Dr. Johnson could have been with us in the Y.M.C.A. from last December to the day of big things! It would have spoilt the standing joke of his life.

In the jaunty bonnet that cast no shadow on the bronzed face underneath, with the warm tints of their tartans between neat tunic and weather-beaten knees, their mere presence lit up the scene; and to scrape acquaintance with one at random was nearly always to tap a character worthy of the outer man. There are those who insist that the discipline of the Army destroys individuality; it may seem so in the transition stage of training, but the nearer the firing-line the less I found it to be the case. I knew a Canadian missioner, turned Coldstream Guardsman, who was very strong and picturesque upon the point.

'Out here,' said he, 'a man goes naked; he can't hide what he really is; he can't camouflage himself.'

The Jock does not try. In the life school of the war he stands stripped, but never poses; sometimes rugged and unrefined; often massive and majestic in body and mind; always statuesque in his simplicity, always the least self-conscious of Britons. Two of his strongest point are his education and his religion, but he makes no parade of either, because both are in his blood. His education is as old as the least humorous of the Johnsonian jibes, as old as the Dominie and the taws: a union that bred no 'brittle intellectuals,' but hard-headed men who have helped the war as much by their steadfast outlook as by their zest and prowess in the field. As for their religion, it is the still deeper strain, mingled as of old with the fighting spirit of this noble race. It is most obvious in the theological students, even the full-fledged ministers, to be found in the ranks of the Jocks to-day; but I have seen it in rougher types who know nothing of their own sleeping fires, who are puzzled themselves by the blaze of joy they feel in battle and will speak of it with characteristic frankness and simplicity.

'The pleasure it gives ye! The pleasure it gives ye!' said one who had been breathing wonders about their ding-dong, hand-to-hand bomb-and-bayonet work. 'This warr,' he went on to declare, 'will do more for Christianity than ever was done in the wurruld before.'

This also he reiterated, and then added surprisingly:

'Mine ye, I'm no' a Christian mysel'; but this warr will do more for Christianity than ever was done in the wurruld before.'

The personal disclaimer was repeated in its turn, in order to remove any possible impression that the speaker was any better than he ought to be. At least I thought that was the explanation; none was offered or indeed invited, for there were other men waiting at the counter; and we never met again, though he promised to come back next night. That boy meant something, though he did not mean me to know how much. He came from Glasgow, talked and laughed like Harry Lauder, and did both together all the time. His conversation made one think. It would be worth recording for its cheery, confidential plunge into deep waters; nobody but a Jock would have taken the first header.

Yet, out of France, the Scottish have a reputation for reserve! Is it that in their thoroughgoing way they strip starker than any, where all go as naked as my Canadian friend declared?

They are said to be (God bless them!) our most ferocious fighters. I should be sorry to argue the point with a patriotic Australian; but my money is on the Jock as the most affectionate comrade. It is a touching thing to hear any soldier on a friend who has fought and fallen at his side; but the poetry that is in him makes it wonderful to hear a Jock; you get the swirl of the pipes in his voice, the bubble of a Highland burn in his brown eyes. So tender and yet so terrible! So human and so justly humorous in their grief!

'He was the best wee Sergeant ever a mon had,' one of them said to me, the night after a costly raid. We have no English word to compare with that loving diminutive; 'little' comes no nearer it than 'Tommy' comes near 'Jock.' One even doubts whether there are any 'wee' Sergeants who do not themselves make use of the word.

I could tell many a moving tale as it was told to me, in an accent that I never adored before. On second thoughts it is the very thing I cannot do and will not attempt. But here is a letter that has long been in my possession; a part of it has been in print before, in a Harrow publication, for it is all about a Harrow boy of great distinction; but this is the whole letter. It makes without effort a number of the points I have been labouring; it throws a golden light on the relations between officers and men in a famous Highland Regiment; but its unique merit lies in the fact that it was not written for the boy's people to read. It is a Jock's letter to a Jock, about their officer:—

'FRANCE, 1. 9. 15.

DEAR TOMMY,—

Just a note to let you know that I am still alive and kicking. Things are much the same as when you left here. We have had one good kick up since you were wounded, that was on the 9th of May. We lost little Lieut. —, the best man that ever toed the line. You know what like he was; the arguments you and him used to have about politics. He always said you should have been Prime Minister. None of the rest of them ever mixed themselves with us the same as he done; he was a credit to the regiment and to the father and mother that reared him; and Tommy the boys that are left of the platoon hopes that you will write to his father and mother and let them know how his men loved him, you can do it better than any of us. I enclose you a cutting out of a paper about his death. He died at the head of his platoon like the toff he was, and, Tommy, I never was very religious but I think little — is in Heaven. He knew that it was a forlorn hope before we were half way, but he never flinched. He was not got for a week or two after the battle. Well, dear chum, I got your parcel and am very thankful for it. I will be getting a furlough in a week or two and I will likely come and see you, not half. All the boys that you knew are asking kindly for you. We are getting thinned out by degrees. There are 11 of us left of the platoon that you know—some dead, some down the line. But Tommy we miss you for your arguments, and the old fiddle was left at Parides, nobody to play it; but still we are full of life. I expect you will read some of these days of something big. I may tell you the Boches will get hell for leather before they are many days older. We have the men now and the material and we won't forget to lay it on. Old Bendy is major now, he gave us a lecture a while ago and he had a word to say about you and wee Hughes and Martin, that was the night that you went to locate the mortar and came in with the machine gun. He says the three of you were a credit to the regiment. I just wish you were back to keep up the fun, but your wife and bairns will like to keep you now. Well, Tommy, see and write to —'s father and let him know how his men liked him, it will perhaps soften the blow. No more now, but I remain your ever loving chum and well wisher, SANDY.

'Good night and God bless you.

'P.S.—Lochie Rob, J. Small, Philip Clyne, Duncan Morris, Headly, wee Mac, Ginger Wilson, Macrae and Dean Swift are killed. There are just three of us left in the section now, that is, Gordon, Black, and Martin, the rest drafted.

'Write soon.'

Thomas himself is not quite so simple. He is not writing as man to man, but to an intermediary who will show every word to 'little —'s' family. He is not speaking just for himself, but for his old platoon, and added to this responsibility is the manly duty of keeping up his own repute, both as one who 'should have been Prime Minister' and as one who 'can do it better than any of us.' Thomas is somewhere or other in hospital, but for all his hurts there are passages of his that come from squared elbows and a very sturdy pen:

'He was young so far as years were concerned, but he was old in wisdom. He never asked one of us to do that which he would not do himself. He shared our hardships and our joys. He was in fact one of ourselves as far as comradeship and brotherly love was concerned. We never knew who he was till we saw his death in the Press, but this we did know, that he was Lieut. —, a gentleman and a soldier every inch, and mind you the average Tommy is not too long in getting the size of his officer, and it is not every day that one like — joins the Army....

He was liked by his fellow-officers, but he was loved, honoured and respected by his men, and you know, Sir, that I am not guilty of paying tributes to anyone where they are not deserved....'

I love Thomas for the two italicised asides. It was not he who underlined them; but they declare his politics as unmistakably as Sandy's bit about those arguments with their officer. For 'little —' was the son of one of Scotland's noblest and most ancient houses; but Thomas is careful to explain that they never knew that until the papers told them, and we have internal evidence that Sandy never gave it a thought. He lays no stress on the fact that 'none of the rest of them ever mixed themselves with us the same as he done': the gem of both tributes, when you come to think of it.

I think of it the more because I knew this young Harrovian a little in his brilliant boyhood (Head of the School and Captain of the Football Eleven), but chiefly because I happen to have seen his grave. It is on the outskirts of a village that was still pretty and wooded in early '17, though the church was in a bad way even then. Now there can be little left; but I hope against hope that some of the wooden crosses which so impressed me are still intact. For there as ever among his men, I think even alongside 'wee Mac' and the others named in that pathetic postscript, lies 'little —', truly 'mixing himself with them' to the last.

In the same row, under mound and cross as neat as any, lay 'an unknown German soldier'; and for his sake, perhaps, if all have not been blown to the four winds, the present occupiers[1] will do what can be done to protect and preserve the resting-place of 'little —' and his Jocks.

[Footnote 1: July, 1918.]

GUNNERS

Next to the Jocks, I used to find the Gunners the cheeriest souls about a hut. Nor do I believe that mine was a chance experience; for the constant privilege of inflicting damage on the Hun must be, despite a very full share of his counter-attentions, a perpetual source of satisfaction. A Gunner is oftener up and doing, far seldomer merely suffering, than any other being under arms. The Infantry have so much to grin and bear, so very much that would be unbearable without a grin, that it is no wonder if the heroic symbol of their agony be less in evidence upon ordinary occasions. Cheeriness with them has its own awful connotation: they are almost automatically at their best when things are at their worst; but the gunner is always enjoying the joke of making things unpleasant for the other side. He is the bowler who is nearly certain of a good match.

He used to turn up at our hut at all hours, sometimes in a Balaclava helmet that reminded one of other winter sports, often with his extremities frozen by long hours in the saddle or on his limber, but never wearied by much marching and never in any but the best of spirits. He was always an interesting man, who knew the Line as a strolling player knows the Road, but neither knew nor cared where he was to give the next performance. I associate him with a ruddy visage and a hearty manner that brought a breeze in from the outer world, as a good stage sailor brings one from the wings.

One great point about the Gunners is that you can see them at their job. I had seen them at it on a former brief visit to the front, and even had a foretaste of their quality of humour, which is by no means so heavy as a civilian wag might apprehend. The scene was the tight-rope road between Albert and Bapaume, then stretched across a chasm of inconceivable devastation, and only three-parts in our hands; in fact we were industriously shelling Bapaume and its environs when a car from the Visitors' Château dumped two of us, attended by a red-tabbed chaperon, in the very middle of our guns.

Not even in later days do I remember such a row as they were making. Shells are as bad, but I imagine one does not hear a great many quite so loud and live to write about it. Drum-fire must be worse at both ends; but I have heard only distant drum-fire, and on the spot it must have this advantage, that its continuity precludes surprise. But a series of shattering surprises was the essence of our experience before Bapaume. The guns were all over the place, and fiendishly camouflaged. I was prepared for all sorts of cunning and picturesque screens and emplacements, and indeed had looked for them. I was not prepared for absolutely invisible cannon of enormous calibre that seemed to loose off over our shoulders or through our legs the moment our backs were turned.

If you happened to be looking round you were all right. You saw the flash, and your eye forewarned your ear in the fraction of a second before the bang, besides reassuring you as to the actual distance between you and the blazing gun; but whenever possible it took a mean advantage, and had me ducking as though somebody had shouted 'Heads!' I say 'me,' not before it was time; for I can only speak with honesty for myself. By flattering chance I was pretending to enjoy this experience in good company indeed; but the great man might have been tramping his own moor, and doing the shooting himself, for all the times I saw his eyelids flicker or his massive shoulders wince. He made no more of a howitzer that jovially thundered and lightened in our path, over our very heads, than of the brace of sixty-pounders whose peculiarly ear-destroying duet 'scratched the brain's coat of curd' as we stood only too close behind them. They might have been a brace of Irish Members for all their intimidatory effect on my illustrious companion.

But the fun came when we adjourned to the Battery Commander's dug-out, and somebody suggested that the Forward Observing Officer would feel deeply honoured by a word on the telephone from so high an Officer of State. All urbanity, the O.S. took down the receiver, and was heard introducing himself to the F.O.O. by his official designation, as though high office alone could excuse such a liberty. The receiver cackled like a young machine-gun, and the O.S. beamed dryly on the O.C.

'He wants to know who the devil I really am!' he reported with due zest.

Hastily the spectacled young Major vouched for the other speaker. The receiver changed hands once more. The Forward Observing Officer was evidently as good as his style and title.

'He says—"in that case"—I'd better look him up!' twinkled the O.S. 'Is there time? He says he's quite close to the sugar factory.'

The sugar factory was unmistakable, not as a flagrant sugar factory but as the only fragment of a building left standing within the sky-line. It proved a snare. Our F.O.O. was unknown there; if he had ever been at the ex-factory, he had kept himself to himself and gone without leaving an address; and though we sought him high and low among the shell-holes, under the belching muzzles of our guns, it was not intended by Providence (nor yet peradventure by himself) that we should track that light artillery comedian to his place of concealment.

Still, one can get at a gunner (in the above sense only) quicker than at any other class of acquaintance in the Line.

It is, after all, a very small war in the same sense as it is said to be a small world; and in our ruined town I was always running into some soldier whom I had known of old in leather or prunella. I have had the pleasure of serving an old servant as an impressive N.C.O., of welcoming others of all ranks on both sides of the counter. Thus it was that one day I had a car lent me to go pretty well where I liked, subject to the approval of a young Staff Officer, my escort. I thought of a Gunner friend hidden away somewhere in those parts. He was an Old Boy of my old school. So, as it happened, was the High Commander to whom the car belonged; so, by an extraordinary chance, was the young Staff Officer. The oldest of them, of course, long years after my time; but an All Uppingham Day for me, if ever I had one! I only wish we could have claimed the hero of the day as well.

The car took us to within a couple of miles of my friend, who was not above another mile from No-Man's Land. It was a fairly lively sector at the best of times, which was about the time I was there. The enemy had shown unseasonable activity only the night before, and we met some of the casualties coming down a light railway, up which we walked the last part of the way. Two or three khaki figures pushing a truck laden with a third figure—supine, blanketed, and very still: that was the picture we passed several times in the thin February sunlight. One man looked as dead as the livid landscape; one had a bloody head and a smile that stuck; one was walking, supported by a Red Cross man, coughing weakly as he went. Round about our destination were a number of shell-sockets, very sharp and clean, all made in the night.

It was quite the deepest dug-out I was ever in, but I was not sorry when I had found my eyes in the twilight of its single candle. Warm, down there; a petrol engine throbbing incomprehensibly behind a curtain at the foot of the flight; a ventilating shaft at the inner end; hardly any more room than in an Uppingham study. How we talked about the old place, three school generations of us, sitting two on a bed until I broke down the Major's! The Major might have been bored before that—he who alone had not been there. But even my ponderous performance did not disturb a serene forbearance, a show of more than courteous interest, which encouraged us to persist in that interminable gossip about masters (with imitations!) so maddening to the uninitiated. At length the petrol engine stopped; I doubt if we did, though steak and onions now arrived. May I never savour their crude smell again without remembering that time and place; the oftener the better, if there be those present who do not know about the Major.

His second-in-command, my Uppingham friend, told me as he saw us along the light railway on our way back. In 1914 the Major had been a Nonconformist Minister. Never mind the Denomination, or the part of Great Britain: because the Call sounded faint there, and his flock were slow to answer, the shepherd showed the way, himself enlisting in the ranks: because he was what he was, and came whence he came, here and thus had I found him in 1918, commanding a battery on the Somme, at the age—but that would be a tale out of school. A legion might be made up of the men whose real ages are nobody's business till the war is over; then they might be formed into a real Old Guard of Honour, and splendidissime mendax might be their motto.

I do not say the Major would qualify. I have forgotten exactly what it was I heard upon the point. But I am not going to forget something that reached me later from another source altogether, namely the lips of a sometime N.C.O. of the Battery.

'There was not,' he asserted, 'better discipline in any battery in France. But not a man of us ever heard the Major swear.'

It was a great friend of mine that I had gone forth to see: a cricketer whose only sin was the century that kept him out of the pavilion: a man without an enemy but the one he turned out to fight at forty. Yet the man I am gladdest to have seen that day on the Somme is not my friend, but my friend's friend and Major.... And to think that he opened his kindly fire upon me by saying absurd things about the only book of mine which has very many friends; and that I let him, God forgive me, instead of bowing down before the gorgeous man!

THE GUARDS

The Jocks started me thinking in units, the Gunners set me off on the chance meetings of this little war, and between them they have taken me rather far afield from my Noah's Ark in the mud. But I am not going back just yet, though the ground is getting dangerous. I am only too well aware of that. It is presumptuous to praise the living; and I for one would rather stab a man in the back than pat him on it; but may I humbly hope that I do neither in these notes? The bristling risks shall not deter me from speaking of marvellous men as I found them, nor yet from expressing as best I may the homage they inspired. I can only leave out their names, and the names of the places where we met, and trust that my precautions are not themselves taken in vain. But there is no veiling whole units, or at least no avoiding some little rift within the veil. And when the unit is the Guards—but even the Guards were not all in one place last winter.

Enough that at one time there were Guardsmen to be seen about the purlieus of that 'battered caravanserai' which the war found an antique city of sedate distinction, and is like to leave yet another scrap-heap. The Guards were in the picture there, if not so much so as the Jocks; for in kilt and bonnet the Jocks on active service are more like Jocks than the Guards are like Guardsmen; nevertheless, and wherever they wander, the Guards are quite platitudinously unlike any other troops on earth.

Memorable was the night they first swarmed into my first hut. 'Debouched,' I daresay, would be the more becoming word; but at any rate they duly marched upon the counter, in close order at that, and (as the correspondents have it) 'as though they had been on parade.' Few of them had anything less than a five-franc note; all required change; soon there was not a coin in the till. I wish the patronesses of Grand Clearance Sales could have seen how the Guards behaved that night. Not one of them showed impatience; not one of them was inconsiderate, much less impolite; the sanctity of the queue could not have been more scrupulously observed had our Labour boy been there to see to nothing else. He was not there, and I sighed for him when there was time to sigh; for it was easily the hardest night's work I had in France. But the Guards did their best to help us; they were always buying more than they wanted, 'to make it even money'; continually prepared to present the Y.M.C.A. with the change we could not give them. Never was a body of men in better case—calmer, more immaculate, better-set-up, more dignified and splendid to behold. They might have walked across from Wellington Barracks; they were actually fresh from what I have heard them call 'the Cambrai do.'

There was a bitterly cold night a little later on; it was also later in the night. My young chief was already a breathing pillar of blankets. I was still cowering over a reddish stove, thinking of the old hot-water bottle which was even then preparing a place for my swaddled feet: from outer darkness came the peculiar crunch of heavy boots—many pairs of them—rhythmically planting themselves in many inches of frozen snow. I went out and interviewed a Guards' Corporal with eighteen eager, silent file behind him, all off a leave train and shelterless for the night, unless we took them in. I pointed out that we had no accommodation except benches and trestle-tables, and the bare boards of the hut, where the stove had long been black and the clean mugs were freezing to their shelf.

'We shall be very satisfied,' replied the Corporal, 'to have a roof over us.'

I can hear him now: the precise note of his appreciation, candid yet not oppressive: the dignified, unembittered tone of a man too proud to make much of a minor misfortune of war. Yet for fighting-men just back from Christmas leave, howsoever it may have come about, what a welcome! I never felt a greater brute than lying warm in my bed, within a yard of the stove that still blushed for me, and listening to those silent men taking off their accoutrements with as little noise as possible, preparing for a miserable night without a murmur. Later in the winter, it was said that men were coming back from leave disgruntled and depressed. My answer was this story of the Corporal and the eighteen freezing file. But they were Guardsmen nearly all.

Not the least interesting of individual Guardsmen was one who across our counter nicely and politely declared himself an anarchist. It was the slack hour towards closing-time, before the National Anthem at the cinema prepared us for the final influx, and I am glad I happened to be free to have that chat. It was most instructive. My Guardsman, who was accompanied by the inevitable Achates, was not a temporary soldier; both were fine, seasoned men of twelve or thirteen years' service, who had been through all the war, with such breaks as their tale of wounds had necessitated. The anarchist did all the talking, beginning (most attractively to me) about cricket. He was a keen watcher of the game, an old habitué of Burton Court and intense admirer of certain distinguished performers for the Household Brigade. 'A great man!' was his concise encomium for more than one. How the anarchy came in I have forgotten. It was decked in dark sayings of a rather homely cut, concerning the real war to follow present preliminaries; but I thought the real warrior was himself rather in the dark as to what it was all to be about. At any rate he failed to enlighten me, as perhaps I failed to enlighten him on the common acceptation of the term 'anarchy.' Reassure me he did, however, by several parenthetical observations, which seemed to fall from the inveterate soldier rather than the soi-disant revolutionary.

'But of course we shall see this war through first,' he kept interrupting himself to impress on me. 'Nothing will be done till we have beaten Germany.'

On balance I was no wiser about the anarchist point of view, but all the richer for this peep into a Guardsman's mind. It was like a good sanitary cubicle filled with second-hand gimcrackery, but still the same good cubicle, still in essentials exactly like a few thousand more. The meretricious jumble was kept within rigid bounds of discipline and good manners, and not as a temporary measure either; for I was solemnly assured that the 'real war,' when it came, would be a bloodless one. Let us hope other incendiaries will adopt my friend's somewhat difficult ideal of an ordered anarchy! As for his manners, I can only say I have heard views with which I was in full personal agreement made more offensive by a dogmatic advocate than were these monstrous but quite amiable nebulosities. If anarchy is to come, I know which anarchist I want to 'ride in the whirlwind and direct the storm'; he will spare Burton Court, I do believe; and even catch himself saluting, with true Guards' élan, the 'great men' who are still permitted to hit out of it.

Tradition in the Guards, you conjecture, means more than machine-guns, more than artillery support; it is half the battle they are always pulling out of the fire. It may be other things as well. I heard a delightful story about one Battalion—but I heard it from a fellow-tradesmen whose business it is (or was, before the war) to say more than his prayers. The libel, for it is too good to be true, was that one of the senior Battalions, having given a dinner in some Flemish town early in the war, did a certain amount of inadvertent damage to municipal property during the subsequent proceedings. One in authority wrote to apologise to the maire, enclosing the wherewithal for reparation: whereupon the maire presented himself in high glee, brandishing an equally handsome apology for the same thing done in the same place by the same Regiment in—1711!

One royal night I had myself as the guest of a Company in another of their Battalions. The camp was about half-way between our hut and the front line, near the road and in mud enough to make me feel at home. But whereas we weltered in a town-locked pool, this was in the open sea; not a tree or a chink of masonry in sight; just a herd of 'elephants' or Nissen huts, linked up by a network of duck-boards like ladders floating in the mud. Mud! It was more like clotted cocoa to a mind debauched by such tipple, and the great split tubes of huts like a small armada turned turtle in the filth.

The outer tube I think was steel—duly corrugated—but wooden inner tubes made the mess-hut and the one I shared with my host voluptuously snug and weather-proof. It was the wildest and wettest night of all the winter, but not a drop or a draught came in anywhere, and I am afraid I thought with selfish satisfaction of the many perforations in our own thin-skinned hut. An open fire was another treat to me; and I remember being much intrigued by a buttery-hatch in the background. It reminded me of the third act of The Admirable Crichton.

There were only four of us at dinner, or five including a parrot who hopped about saying things I have forgotten. All the other three were temporary Guardsmen; that I knew; but to me they seemed the lineal descendants of the bear-skinned and whiskered heroes in old volumes of Punch. I suppose they were colder in their Balaclava huts, but I warrant the other atmosphere was much the same. We should not have had Wagner on a gramophone before Sebastopol; but they would have given me Veuve Cliquot, or whatever the very best may have been in those days; and if I had committed the solecism of asking for more bread, having consumed my statutory ration, the mess-waiter of 1855 would have put me right in the same solicitous undertone that spared my blushes in 1918. The perfect blend of luxury and discipline would have been as captivating then as now and ever, and the kindness of my hosts a thing to write about in fear and trembling, no matter how gratefully.

But there would have been no duck-boards to follow through wind and rain to my host's warm hut, and I should not be looking back upon as snug a winter's night as one could wish to spend. How we lay talking while the storm frittered its fury upon the elephant's tough hide! Once more it was talk of schooldays, but not of mine; it was all about Eton this time, and nearly all about a boy there who had been most dear to us both. He was now out here in his grave; but which of them was not? Of the group that I knew best before the war, only he whom I was with to-night! I lay awake listening to his even breathing, and prayed that he at least might survive the holocaust yet to come.

A BOY'S GRAVE

Somewhere in Flanders there was a ruined estaminet, with an early trench running round it, that I longed to see for the sake of a grave in a farm-yard not far behind. The grave itself was known to be obliterated. Though dug very deep by men who loved the boy they laid there at dead of night, and though the Sergeant (who loved him most) could say what a strong cross they had placed over it, the grave was so situated, and the whole position so continuously under fire, that official registration was never possible, nor any further reassurance to be had. The boy's Division went out of the Line, and at length went back into another sector; but more than one officer who knew his people, and one brave friend who had only heard of them, searched the spot without avail. For two years it was so near the enemy and so heavily shelled that the fear became a moral certainty that everything had been swept away; then the boy's father chanced to meet his Army Commander; and that great human soldier ordered the investigation that bore out every dread. Nothing remained to mark the grave. And yet I longed to see the place; the tide of battle had at last receded; at least I might see what was left of the trench where the boy had fallen, and have something to tell his mother on my return. So I had set my heart, originally, on working for the Y.M.C.A. in Flanders. Had I been given my way about that, very little that I have now to tell could possibly have happened.

It was ordained, however, that I should go to France, and a long way down the Line, an impossible journey from my secret goal. To be honest, I had a voice in this myself, and even readily acquiesced in the arrangement; for there were sound reasons for taking the first opening that offered; and on reflection I saw myself the unsoundness of my first position. After all, I was not going out for secret or for private ends; and even in Flanders, what means or what authority should I have had for hunting among graves, marked or unmarked? What guide could I have hoped to get to show me all I wished to see, and what could I have seen or done without a guide? Already the new plan spelt a providential exclusion from a sphere of futile mortification and divided desires: to France I went, and with an easy mind. And in France the first people I saw, in my first hut, as customers across the counter, were the boy's old Division!

I suppose the odds against that must have been fairly long. Of all the Divisions in the B.E.F. only three were plying between our town and the Line; and of those three that Division was one. It was, moreover, the one that we saw most of in the Ark. Theirs were the pink barracks just outside our gates; it was their cinema that lay across our bows in the mud; their motley Battalions that could make the hut a Babel of all the dialects in Great Britain. The boy's Brigade was up the Line when I arrived; in a few days it came down, and under the familiar regimental cap-badge how eagerly I sought the faces that looked old enough to have three years' service! They are the veterans of this war; but few, it seemed, were left. Did I discover one, he had not been in B Company. I grew ashamed of questioning. It was not before the Brigade had been up the Line for another sixteen days, and come back again, that a little hard-bitten man aroused fresh hopes and passed all tests. He had not only been in the Regiment at the time, but in B Company; not only in B Company, but in the boy's Platoon; there when he fell; one of the burial party!

We had a long talk in the inner room. It appeared there were two other survivors of the old Platoon; the Sergeant, as I knew to my sorrow, had died Company Sergeant-Major at Passchendaele. Of the other two, one in particular, now a bandsman but in 1915 a stretcher-bearer, could tell me everything: he should come and see me himself. He never did come, and I saw no more of the little man who promised to send him. Once again they all went up the Line, and by the time that tour was over I had deserted the hut near their barracks. The little man called there and left a message; it was to say he was going on leave for three weeks, and the Battalion were going away to rest. When they all got back, he would bring the bandsman to see me without fail.

It is a long story; but then Coincidence (or what we will) was stretching a very long arm. Coincidence (at least in the literal sense) was indeed stretching out both arms: one of them was busy all this time at distant Ypres. An unknown friend there, remotely connected with the boy's people, thought he had discovered the boy's grave. He had written home to say so; the news was sent out to me, and we got into correspondence. He had searched the shell-blasted farm-yard where the burial was known to have taken place, and he had discovered—evidence. Some of this evidence he eventually sent me: a cheap French or Flemish watch, red with the rust and mould of a soldier's grave: just the watch that a boy would buy at the nearest town for his immediate needs. Now, at the time of his death, this boy's watch was being mended in London; therefore, the one now in my hands was good evidence as far as it went. A boot-strap had been found as well, and something else that tallied terribly; on the strength of all this testimony, and of an instinctive certainty in the mind of our unknown friend, a new cross already marked the site of these discoveries. He wanted me to see the place for myself, and as soon as possible, in case the enemy should make his expected thrust in that quarter. Nor could I have gone too soon for my own satisfaction. Grave or no grave (for I could not quite share his sanguine conviction), I longed to grasp the hand of a man who had done so much for people he had never met: and to see all there was to see with my own eyes.

But it is not so easy to travel sixty miles up or down the Line. It is a question of permits, which take some getting, and of facilities which very properly do not exist. Military railways are not for the transport of civilian camp-followers on private business; moreover, they do go slow when there is no military occasion for much speed; and I had my work, when all was said. But my luck (if you like) was in again. The first old friend that I had met in France was a friend in a higher place than I may say. Already he had shown himself my friend indeed; now, in my need—But here the coincidences multiply, and must be kept distinct.

On the very morning I heard from Ypres—with the watch and the invitation—I was due to visit this old friend in another part altogether. He sent his car for me, the splendid man. I showed him my letter from Ypres.

'You will have to go,' he said.

'But how?'

'In my car.'

'Sixty miles!'

(It was much more from where he was.)

'You can have it for two days.'

I could not thank him; nor can I here. How can a man speak for the mother of an only child, whose grave he was to see with her eyes as well as with his own, so that one day he might tell her all? Without a car, in fine, the thing was impossible. There are no thanks for actions such as this: none that words do not belittle. A day was fixed, ten days ahead; this gave me time to write to the boy's mother, and gave her time to send direct to Ypres all the bulbs and plants that she could get, to make her child's bed as gay that spring as he himself had been all the days they were together.

And yet—and yet—was it his grave that had been found? Was the evidence as good as it seemed? I was going all the way to Ypres on the strength of that local evidence only. If I could but have taken one or other of those two men who were there when it happened in 1915! But one of them was away on leave, his three weeks not nearly up; the other, the bandsman who knew most of all, might or might not be with the Battalion; but the Battalion itself was still away. I found that out for certain on the morning of the day before I was to start. They were still resting many kilometres back. I had no means of getting to them, even if I had had the right sort of desire; but the fact was that everything had come about so beautifully without one move of mine, that I was quite consciously content to drift in the current of an unfathomable influence.

That afternoon there came to my hut, for no particular reason that he ever told me, a man I had not met before. He was the Senior Chaplain of the boy's Division. We made friends, by what steps I cannot remember, but I must have told him where I was going next day. He was interested. I told him the whole thing. He said: 'But surely there must be somebody in the Battalion that you could take with you, to identify the place?' I told him there was such a man, a bandsman, but the Battalion was away resting and I was not sure but that the man himself was on leave. Said the Chaplain: 'I can find out. I know where they are. I can get them on the telephone. If you don't hear from me again, go round their way in the morning when you get the car. It's ten kilometres in the wrong direction, but it may be worth your while.'

Worth my while! I did not hear from him again; not a word all that anxious evening to spoil the prospect he had opened up; and in the morning came the car, a powerful limousine, mine for the next two days! My pass from the A.P.M. was for Ypres only, but I did not think of that. In less than an hour we had found those rest-billets among ploughed fields at peace in the spring sunshine; and at the right regimental headquarters, a young Corporal ready waiting in his field overcoat. It was the bandsman: he who had been nearest to the boy at the very last, to whose special care his dear body had been committed. The living man who had most to tell me!

And the first thing he told me showed what a mercy it was to have him with me; but at the moment it came as a shock. I had shown him the watch; he had shaken his head. No watch had been buried with the boy; of that the Corporal was unshakably certain; and he was the man to know, the man whose duty it had been to make sure at the time. Away went our strongest piece of evidence! Then I told him about the boot-strap, always a doubtful item in my own mind; and the Corporal swept it aside at once. The boy had not worn boots with straps; he had worn ordinary laced boots and puttees; exactly as I had been thinking at the back of my mind. He had not been out many weeks, and I knew every noble inch of him that went away. So, after all, it was not his grave that had been found! That would have been a grievous blow but for the transcending thought—it was not his grave that had been disturbed! And we might never have known but for this young soldier at my side who was saying quite confidently that he could show me where the grave really was! One of—at most—three living men who could!

Who had brought him to my side—at the last moment—the very man I wanted—the one man needful?

To be sure, the Senior Chaplain of their Division; but why should the Senior Chaplain, a man I never saw before, have come to my hut in the nick of time to do me this service, so definitely desired? Why should I myself have come to the very place in France where the Division was waiting for me—the one place where I had also an old friend with a car to lend me when the time came? Why had I not gone to Belgium (to be near the boy) as I at first intended? And why, at that very time, should a complete stranger have been making entirely independent efforts to find the grave in Belgium that I yearned to see?

'Chance' is no answer, unless the word be held to cover an organic tissue of chances, each in turn closely related to some other chance, all component parts of a chance whole! And what sensation novelist would build a plot on such foundations and hope to make his tale convincing? Not I, at my worst; and there were more of these chances still to come, albeit none that mattered as did those already recounted.

Nor is there very much left to tell that bears telling here. In Ypres I did not find my great unknown friend; he had warned me, when it was too late to alter plans, that he might be called home on a private matter; and this had happened. But he had told me I should find his 'trusty Sergeant,' who had taken part in the investigations, ready to help me in every way; and so, indeed, I did. The man was, among other things, an enthusiastic amateur gardener; he had known exactly what to do with the bulbs and plants, which he had unpacked on their arrival and was keeping nice and moist for next morning. But this was not the first thing we had to talk about. The first thing was to impress upon the Sergeant the importance of not letting my witness know that a new cross had been put up, and so to ensure absolutely independent identification of the spot. He gave me his promise, and I know he kept it.

Next morning, under a leaden February sky, the three of us drove north in the car, accompanied by a second Sergeant with digging tools, in case the bandsman located the grave elsewhere and I was bent upon some proof. At the time I did not know why he was with us; later, the quiet little fact above spoke volumes for the good faith of the party. It was completed by a young Catholic Padre from Ypres, so that the only office which the boy had lacked at the hands of his dear men might now be fulfilled.

I am following the course we took upon a military map given to the boy's father by one of the many officers who had befriended him in his trouble; and I had been prepared for the thickening cluster of shell-holes further on by more than one aeroplane photograph sent from Army Headquarters. O that all whom this war has robbed of their hearts' delight could know, as this father knows, how the huge heart of the Army is with them in their sorrow! There was the Army Commander, who had done what he could for a man he met but once by chance; it was not much that even he could do, but how more than readily it had been done! And now here in the car, itself a tangible sign of infinite compassion, were these N.C.O.'s and this young priest, with their grave faces and their kind eyes! One's heart went out to them. It seemed all wrong to be taking men, who any day might be in theirs, to see a soldier's grave in cold blood. So we fell to discussing the sky, the mud, and such landmarks as remained, quite simply and naturally, as the boy himself would have wished.

'Plains that the moonlight turns to sea,' the boy had quoted in describing the plain we were crossing now; but it had become a broken plain since his time; covered with elephant huts and pill-boxes, scored by light railways; the roads on which no man might live in those days, themselves alive with traffic in these, with lorries and men and all the abundant activities of a host behind a host. The car stopped one or two hundred yards from our destination, towards which we threaded our way over duck-boards, through and past these mushroom habitations, till we came to the green open space which was all that remained of the farm. Not a stone or a brick to be seen; not even a heap of bricks, or a charred beam, or the empty socket of pillar or post; only the two gate-posts themselves, looking like the stumps of trees. But what better than a gateway to give a man his bearings? It led the bandsman straight to a regular file of such stumps, which really had been trees: and in his path stood a white cross, new and sturdy, at which I had been looking all the time: at which he stopped without looking twice, still studying the ground and the bits of landmarks that survived. It was the place.

It was the boy's grave; and the discoverer's—nay, the diviner's—instinct stood vindicated as wonderfully as his evidence had been discredited. Almost adjoining it was a great shell-hole full of water; but it was not our grave that the shell had rifled. Our grave had been dug too deep. It was as though the boy himself had said: 'It's my grave all right—but I don't want you to go thinking those were my things! All that was me or mine is just as they left it.'

So we took off our helmets and stood listening to the young priest reading the last office, in Latin first and then in English. And many of the beautiful sentences were punctuated by loud reports, which I took for our guns if I thought of them at all; for as yet I had heard hardly anything else down south; but after the service I saw little black balloons appearing by magic in mid-air, expanding into dingy cloudlets, and presently dissolving shred by shred. It was enemy shrapnel all the time.

Then the two Sergeants prepared the ground with gentle skill; and we knelt and put in the narcissus bulbs, the primroses and pinks, the phlox and the saxifrage, that the boy's mother had sent him; and a baby rose-tree from an old friend who loved him, in the corner of England that he loved best; it must be climbing up his cross, if it has lived to climb at all.

The clouds had broken before the service ended with the sprinkling of Holy Water; and now between the shell-bursts, while we were yet busy planting, came strains of distant music, as thin and faint and valiant as the February sunshine. It was one of our British bands, perhaps at practice in some safe fold of the famous battle-field, more likely assisting at some ceremonial further away than I imagined; for they seemed to be playing very beautifully; and when they finished with 'Auld Lang Syne' they could not have hung more pathetically upon the closing bars if they had been playing at our graveside, for the boy who always loved a band.

Then there was his trench to see; but it was full of water where it had not fallen in, and was not like a trench any more. And the estaminet at the cross-roads, that cruelly warm corner whence he passed into peace, it too had vanished from the earth. But the gentle slope that had been No-Man's Land was much as he must have seen it in anxious summer dawns, and under the stars that twinkled on so many of his breathless adventures in the early bombing days, when he pelted Germans in their own trench with his own hand, and thought it all 'a jaunt'; thought it 'just like throwing in from cover'; declared it 'as safe as going up to a man's front door-bell—pulling it—and running off again!'

Well, this was where he had played those safe games; and true enough, it was not by them he met his death, but standing-to down there under shell-fire, on a summer's morning after his own heart, with eyes like the summer sky turned towards the same line of trees my eyes were beholding now, his last thought for his men. I could almost hear his eager question:

'Is everybody all right?'

They were the boy's last words.

Did I enter into the spirit of all that last chapter of his dear life the better for being on the scene, and watching shrapnel burst over it even as he had watched it a thousand times? I cannot say I did. I doubt if I could have entered into it more than I always had ... we were such friends. But how he must be entering into the whole spirit of my whole pilgrimage! It was like so much of his old life and mine. Always he knew that he had only to call and I would come to him, at school or wherever he was; many a time I had jumped into a car and gone, though he never did call me in his life. Had he now? ... There was my friend's car waiting, as it might have been once more in the lane opposite 'the old grey Chapel behind the trees.' ... And here were we passengers, a party from the four winds, all brought together by different agencies for the same simple end. Who had brought us? Who had prompted or inspired those directly responsible for our being there? It was not, you perceive, a case of one god from a machine, but of three at the very least. Who had so beautifully arranged the whole difficult thing?

Even to that band! But for 'Auld Lang Syne' one might not take it seriously for a moment; but remembering those searching strains, and the pathos put into them, the early hour, the wild place, the bursting shrapnel, who can help the flash of fancy? Not one who will never forget the boy's gay, winning knack of getting bands to play what he wanted; this was just the tune he would have called, that we might all join hands and not forget him, yet remember cheerily for his sake!

But it all had been as he would have had it if he could: not one little thing like that, but the whole big thing he must have wanted: all granted to him or his without their mortal volition at any stage. Chances or accidents, by the chapter, if you will! No man on earth can prove the contrary; and yet there are few, perhaps, who have lost their all in this war, and who would not thank God for such a string of happenings. But one does not thank God for a chain of chances. And if any link was of His forging, why not the whole chain, as two thankful people dare to think?

THE REST HUT

FRESH GROUND

It was not my inspiration to run one of our huts entirely as a library for the troops. I was merely the fortunate person chosen to conduct the experiment. In most of the huts there was already some small supply of books for circulation, and at our headquarters in the town a dusty congestion of several hundred volumes which nobody had found time to take in hand. The idea was to concentrate these scattered units, to obtain standard reinforcements from London and the base, indent for all the popular papers and magazines, and go into action as a Free Library at the Front. It was at first proposed to do without any kind of a canteen; but I was all against driving a keen reader elsewhere for his tea, and held out for light refreshments after four and cigarettes all the time. On this and many other points I was given my way in a fashion that would have fired anybody to make the venture a success.

The hut placed at my disposal was a very good one in the middle of the town, indeed within the palisade of the once magnificent Town Hall. That grandiose pile had been knocked into mountains of rubbish, with the mere stump of its dizzy belfry still towering over all as the Matterhorn of the range. These ruins formed one side of a square like a mouthful of bad teeth, all hollow stumps or clean extractions; our upstart hut was the only whole building of any sort within sight. It had a better saloon than my last land-ship; on the other hand, it was infested with rats from the surrounding wrecks. They would lope across the floor under one's nose, or dangle their tails from the beams overhead, and I slept with a big stick handy.

Relays of peace-time carpenters, borrowed from their units for a day or two each, fell upon all the benches and table-tops they required, and turned them into five long tiers of book-shelves behind the counter. In the meantime our own Special Artist was busy on a new and noble scheme of decoration, and two or three of us up to our midriffs in the first thousand books. They were a motley herd: the sweepings of unknown benefactors' libraries, the leavings of officers and men, cunning shafts from the devout of all denominations, and the first draft of cheap masterpieces from the base. Classification was beyond me, even if time had been no object: how could one classify 'The Sol of Germany,' 'A Yorkstireman Alroad,' 'The Livinz Waze,' 'From Workhouse to Westminster: Life-Story of With Gooks, M.P.' (four copies), or even the books these titles stood for in the typewritten catalogue that arrived (from Paris) too late to entertain us? All authors in alphabetical order seemed the simplest principle; and in practice even that arrangement ran away with days.

Then each volume had to be labelled (over the publishers' imprint on the binding) and the labels filled in with the letter and number of each in one's least illegible hand; and this took more days, though the rough draft of the catalogue emerged simultaneously; and the merit of the plan, if any, was that the catalogue order eventually coincided with that of the actual books on the shelves. The drawback was that books kept dropping in or turning up too late for insertion in their proper places. I could think of no better way out of this difficulty than by resorting to a large Z class, or dump, for late-comers. This met the case though far from satisfying my instincts for the rigour of a game. Another time (this coming winter, for instance, when I hope to have it all to do again) I shall be delighted to adopt some more approved method of dealing with a growing library; last spring one had to do the best one could by the light of nature. Nevertheless, there was not much amiss (except the handwriting) with the clean copy (in carbon duplicate) of a catalogue which ran to a good many thousand words, and kept two of us out of bed till several successive midnights; for by this time I had a staunch confederate who took the whole thing as seriously as I did, and perhaps even found it as good fun.

We had hoped to open—it was really very like producing a play—early in February, but a variety of vicissitudes delayed the event until the twentieth of the month. As the day approached we had many visitors, who had heard of our effort and were prepared to spread our fame; time was well lost in showing them round, and I confess I enjoyed the job. They had to begin by admiring the scraper. It was perhaps the worst scraper in Europe—I ached for a week from sinking its two uprights into harder chalk with a heavier pick-axe than I thought existed—but it was symbolical. It meant that you could leave the mud of war outside our hut; but I am afraid the first thing to be seen inside was inconsistent with this symbol. It was the complete Daily Mail sketch-map of the Western Front, the different sheets joined together and mounted on the locked door opposite the one in use. The feature of this feature was that the Line was pegged out from top to bottom with the best red-tape procurable in the town. It toned delightfully with the art-green of the sketch-map.

In the ordinary Y.M.C.A. nobody would have seen it! In winter, at any rate, it is dusk at high noon in the ordinary hut, which is lighted only by canvas windows under the eaves. In our hut, however, we had a pair of fine skylights, expressly cut to save our readers' eyes, and glazed with some shimmering white stuff which seemed to increase the light, like a fall of snow, instead of slightly diluting it like the best of glass. The side windows glistened with the same material, so that a dull day seemed to clear up as you entered. Between the skylights stood four trestle tables under one covering of American cloth, whereon the day's papers, magazines and weeklies, were to be displayed club-fashion; the writing tables, likewise in American cloth, were arranged under the side windows; and at an even distance from either end of the fourfold reading table were the two stoves. One stove is the ordinary hut-allowance.

Round each stove ran a ring of canvas and wicker arm-chairs, in which a tired man might read himself to sleep, and between the chairs stood little round tables for his tea and biscuits when he woke. They were garden tables painted for the part, with spidery black legs and bright vermilion tops, and on each a nice new ash-tray (of the least possible intrinsic value, I admit) in further imitation of the club smoking-room. That was the atmosphere I wanted for the body of the hut.

At the platform end we were ready for anything, from itinerant lecturers to the most local preacher, and from hymns to comic songs; the best piano in the area was equal to any strain; and a somewhat portentous rostrum, though not knocked together for me, was just my height, while the American cloth in which we found it was a dead match for our extensive importations of that fabric. It was at this end of the hut that our Special Artist and Decorator had excelled himself. All down the sides were his frieze of flags, his dado of red and white cotton in alternate stripes, and his own extraordinarily effective chalk drawings on sheets of brown paper between the windows. But for the angle under the roof, over the platform, he had reserved his masterpiece. One day, while we were still busy with the books, our handy man of genius had stood for an hour or two on a ladder; and descending, left behind him a complete allegorical cartoon of Literature, including many life-size figures in flowing robes busy with the primitive tools of one's trade. I am not an art critic, like my friend the war correspondent, who ruthlessly detected faults in drawing, instead of applauding all we had to show him; to me, the pride of our walls was at least a remarkable tour de force. The Official Photographer was to have come at a later date to witness if I exaggerate. He left it too long. He may have another chance this winter. 'Literature' has been preserved.

These private views too often started at the counter, because visitors had a way of entering through my room; but to see the library as I do think it deserved seeing, one had to turn one's back upon all I have described, and with a proper piety bear down upon the books. In their five long shelves, each edged and backed with the warm red cotton of the dado, and broken only by my door behind the counter, those thirty yards of good and bad reading were wholly good to see, on our opening day especially, before the first borrower had made the first gap in their serried ranks. There indeed stood they at attention, their labels at the same unwavering height as so many pairs of puttees (except the few I had not affixed myself); and I felt that I, too, had turned a mob into an army.

Immediately over the top row, on a scroll expertly lettered by our Special Illuminator (another of our talented band), its own new motto, from Thomas à Kempis, ran right across the hut:

Without Labour there is no Rest; nor without Fighting can the Victory be Won.

I really think I was as pleased with that, on the morning I thought of it in bed (having just decided to call the hut The Rest Hut), as Thackeray is said to have been when he danced about his bedroom crying—'"Vanity Fair"! "Vanity Fair"! "Vanity Fair"!' But I only once heard a remark upon our motto from the men. 'Well, that's logic anyhow!' said one when he had read it out across the counter. I could have wished for no better comment from a soldier.

Higher still, in the angle of the roof at this end, the flags of the Allies enfolded the Sign of the Rest Hut, which was an adaptation of the Red Triangle. I was having a slightly more elaborate version compressed into a rubber stamp for all literary matter connected with the hut.

The rubber stamp did not arrive in time for the opening; nor had there been time to stick our few rules into more than a few of the books. But I had a paste-pot and a pile of these labels ready on the counter. And since we are going into details, one may as well swing for the whole sheep:—

THE REST HUT LIBRARY (=Y.M.C.A.=)

This book may be taken out on a deposit of =1 franc. which will be returned when the book is brought back.

Books cannot be exchanged more than once daily, and no Reader is entitled to more than one volume at a time.

A book may be kept as long as required: but in each other's interests Readers are begged to return all books as soon as they conveniently can, and in as good order as possible.

Frankly, we flattered ourselves on dispensing with time-limit and fine; and in practice I can commend that revolutionary plan to other amateur librarians. Obviously you are much less likely to get a book back at all if you want more money with it. You shall hear in what circumstances many of ours were to come back, and at what touching trouble to men of whom one can hardly bear to think to-day.

But all the books were not for circulation; a Poetry and Reference Shelf bestrode my end of the counter. Duplicate Poets were to be allowed out like novels; but they were not expected to have many followers. A more outstanding feature, perhaps the apple of the librarian's glasses was the New Book Table, just in front of the counter at the same end. I thought a tableful of really new books would be tremendously attractive to the real readers, that their mere appearance might convey a certain element of morale. So one long day I had spent upon fifteen begging letters to fifteen different publishers—not the same begging letter either, for some of them I knew and some knew me not wisely but too well. On the whole the fifteen played up, and the New Book Table was well and truly spread for the inaugural feast. The novelties were to grace it for a fortnight before going into the catalogue; and we started with quite a brave display. There were travels and biographies, new novels and books of verse, all spick-and-span in their presentation wrappers; and we arranged them most artistically on a gaudy table-cloth that cost thirty francs; with a large cardboard mug (by our Illuminator) warning other mugs off the course. And I think that really is the last of our preparations, unless I mention the receptacles for waste-paper, which proved quite unable to compete against the floor.

They were, I daresay, the most fatuously faddy and elaborate preparations ever made for a library which might be blown sky-high at any moment by a shell. I had not forgotten that none too remote contingency. But it was the last thing I wanted any man to remember from the moment he crossed our threshold. We were just about five miles from the Germans, and I had gone to work exactly as I should in the peaceful heart of England. But that was just where I wanted a man to think himself—until he stepped back into the War.

OPENING DAY

It really was rather like a first night; but there was this intimidating difference, that whereas the worst play in the world draws at least one good house, we were by no means certain of that measure of success. Our venture had been announced, most kindly, in Divisional Orders, as well as verbally at the Y.M. Cinema; but still we knew it was not everybody who believed in us, and that 'a wash-out' had been predicted with some confidence. Even those in authority, who had most handsomely given me my head, were some of them inclined to shake theirs over the result. It was therefore an exciting moment when we opened at two o'clock on the appointed afternoon. There was more occasion for excitement when I had to lock the door for the last time some weeks later; and the two disappointments are not to be compared; but my private cup has seldom filled more suddenly than when I unlocked it with my own hand—and beheld not one solitary man in sight! 'A wash-out' was not the word. It was my Niagara.

At least it looked like it; but after one bad quarter of an hour it turned into a steady trickle of repentant warriors. If the two of us had been holding a redoubt against the enemy, I am not sure that we should have been more delighted to see them than we were. In half an hour the big reading table was surrounded by solemn faces; each of the two stoves had its full circle in the easy chairs; the New Book Table had been discovered, was being thronged, and the best piano in the area yielding real music to the touch of a real pianist. The Rest Hut had started on its short but happy voyage.

Those there were who came demanding candles and boot-polish, and who fled before our softest answers; and there were seekers after billiards who had to be directed elsewhere for their game. I had tipped too many cues at the last hut, and stopped too many games for the further performance of that worse than thankless task, to have the essential quality of the Rest Hut subverted by a billiard-table. The readers, writers, musicians, and above all the weary men, of an Army Corps were the fish for my rod; and we had not been open an hour before I was enjoying good sport, tempered by early misgiving about my flies.

The first book that I connect with a specific inquiry was one that I had certainly failed to order. It was 'anything of Walter de la Mare's'; and I felt a Philistine for having nothing, but a fool for supposing for a moment that I had pitched my hut within the boundaries of Philistia. There might have been a conspiracy to undeceive me on the point without delay. The Poetry Shelf (despite deficiencies so promptly proven) received attention from the start. I forget if it was Mr. de la Mare's admirer who presently took out The Golden Treasury, of which we mercifully had several copies; it was certainly a Jock. I showed him the Shelf, and could have wrung his hand for the tone in which he murmured 'Keats!' It was reverential, awe-stricken and just right. Clearly his Dominie had not abused the taws.

In the meantime I had taken a deposit on three prose volumes. These were they, these the first three authors to cross my counter:

1. George Meredith: The Ordeal of Richard Feverel.

2. Robert Louis Stevenson: Across the Plains.

3. Hilaire Belloc: Mr. Clutterbuck's Election.

As I say, it seemed like a conspiracy—but I swear I was not one of the conspirators! They were—my benefactor already—the pianist, and his friends; three young privates in the R.A.M.C., all afterwards great friends of mine. Of course, this form was too good to be true of the mass; and the particular Field Ambulance to which they belonged was an unusually brainy unit, as I came to know it through many other representatives; but I shall always be grateful to that musical young Meredithian for the start he gave me, and may this mite of acknowledgment meet his spectacles.

On the same opening page of my first day-book, to be sure, a less rarefied level is reached by some comparatively pedestrian stuff, including a work of Mr. Charles Garvice and no fewer than two wastrels 'of my own composure' (as the village organist had it); but my place (though gratifying) was obviously due to an ulterior curiosity; and among the twenty-three books in all that went out that afternoon, there was a further burst of four that went far to restore the higher standard: they were Lorna Doone, My Novel, Nicholas Nickleby and Oliver Twist. The two first fell to Jocks; the Blackmore masterpiece was read forthwith from cover to cover in the trenches, and that Jock came down by special permission for something else as good!

A happy afternoon, and of still happier omen! But I was going to need more 'good stuff'; that was the first hard fact to be faced. I had not reckoned with those eager intellectuals, the young stretcher-bearers who had borne a lantern for the nonce. They were going to bring their friends, and did; and were I to tabulate the books these youths took out between them, in the busy month to come, it would be pronounced, I think, as good a little library as a modern young man, with a sociological bias and a considered outlook, could wish to form. And then there were all the books we hadn't got for them! But these missing friends did more, perhaps, to make friends for the Rest Hut than such as were there to close the subject; for one might be able to suggest something else instead; and the man might have read that already, but his face might lighten at the recollection, and across the counter on our four elbows the pair of us forge that absent book into the first link of friendship.

But any one can gossip about the books he loves, and with a soldier at the front any fool could talk on any topic. So I had it both ways, as one seldom does, according to the saying. It may be that the men who found their pleasure in the Rest Hut were by nature responsive and enthusiastic, and not merely sensitised and refined by the generous fires of constant camaraderie and unselfish suffering. I am speaking of them now only as I found them across that narrow counter, while I deliberately pasted my label of rules inside the cover, and deliberately dabbed my rubber-stamp down on the fly-leaf opposite. I have seen clean into a noble heart between these delaying rites and a meticulous entry in my day-book. It was pain to me when three or four were waiting their turn, and a certain despatch became imperative; it always meant a corresponding period without any work or any friend-making across the counter.

At the short end, beyond the flap (never lowered in the Rest Hut), my friend and mate dispensed the cigarettes and biscuits, and tea made with devoted care by a wrinkled Frenchwoman worth all the Y.M.C.A. orderlies I ever saw, not excepting the two stalwarts at the Ark. The Rest Hut orderly was a smart soldier of the old type, a clever carpenter, and a good cook with large ideas about breakfast. He lived out, did not give us his whole time, and early struck me as a man of mystery; but he was a quick and willing worker who did his part by us. The jewel of the hut's company was my mate. I can only describe him as an Australian Jock, and of the first water on both sides. Twice or thrice rejected in Australia, he had come home to try again and yet again with no better luck; so here he was, with his fine heart and his dry cough, as near the firing-line as he could get 'for the duration.' I may lose a friend for having said so much, yet I have to add that he had taken the whole burden of the till and its attendant accounts (a hut-leader's business) off the shoulders of inexperience. Friends who predicted the worst of me in this connection, and are surprised to see me still outside a defaulter's cell, will please accept the only explanation.

It was a musical tea that opening afternoon, for another of our talented troupe brought the pick of his orchestra from the Association Cinema in the main street hard by; and for an hour it was like the Carlton, with a difference. I wonder what the Carlton could charge for that difference, even at this stage of the war!

Altogether I thought myself the luckiest civilian alive that February afternoon; but my bed of roses had its crumpled leaf. On the fine great cardboard programme for the week (next the map: our Illuminator again), with its cunning slots for moveable amusements, besides that of the Cinema Orchestra there was something about Prayers. That was where I was coming in—on the wrong side of the counter—and as the night advanced it blew a gale inside me. Five minutes before the time, I mounted the platform and made known the worst; and ever afterwards finished the evening by pursuing the same plan, so that all who wished could withdraw, losing only the last five minutes, and no man (I promised them) have anything unpalatable thrust down his throat. I am not sure that it was the most courageous method of procedure; but it was mine, and the men knew where they were. I used to read a few verses, a Vailima Prayer and but one or two more: some men went out, but there was the satisfaction of feeling that those who stayed were in the mood for Prayers.

After the first week or ten days, a third worker came to help us; and he being a minister, I persuaded him to relieve me of this nightly duty, though with a sigh that was not all relief. I always loved reading to the men, but Prayers are shy work for an old layman, and soldiers (if I know them) care less for the deathless composition of a Saint than for the unpremeditated outpouring of the man before their eyes. The minister used to give them all that, perched on a chair in their midst; and he kept a much fuller hut than I at my rostrum of American cloth.

THE HUT IN BEING

I had thought of finishing my account of our opening day with the impressions of a Corporal in the A.S.C., as recorded in his diary that very night. But though the extract reached me in a most delightful way, and though decency would have disqualified the flattering estimate of 'the Superintendent' (as 'a man of cheery temperament'), on examination none of it quite fits in. As description it covers, though with the fleeter pen of youth, ground on which I have already loitered: enough that it was all 'a big surprise' to him: 'a "home from home"' already to one soldier of a literary turn, and likely in his opinion to prove a joy to 'some of the lonely hearts of the lads in khaki.' Q.E.F.

And though it was weeks and months before the Corporal's testimony came to hand, it felt from the beginning as though we really had 'done it.' I say 'it felt,' because there was something in those few thousand cubic feet of air that one could neither see nor hear; something atmospheric, and yet far transcending any atmosphere, whether of the smoking-room or library or what-not, that we had thought to create; for it was something the men had brought with them, nothing that we had ready. Just as they say on the stage that it is the audience who do half the acting, so it was the soldiers who fought half our little battle—and the winning half.

Each of those first days the hut seemed fuller than the day before; more men came early and stayed late; more were to be counted napping round the stoves (as in my rosiest visions) at the same time; more and more books were taken out; and better books, because it was the better-educated men who came flocking in, the intellectual pick of an Army Corps who made our hut their club. If ever a dream came true, if ever a reality excelled an ideal, it was in the wonderful success of our little effort. Little enough, in all conscience; a bubble in the tide of travail; but it is only in little that these delightful flukes come off, and the bubble was soon enough to burst.

In the meantime there were elements of imperfection even in our Rest Hut: one or two things, and on both sides of the counter, to pique a passion for the impeccable.

To begin with the books, we really had not enough Good Stuff. Not nearly! Nor am I thinking only, nor yet chiefly, of Good Stuff in the shape of narrative fiction. It is true that we had not Merediths enough, nor a supply of Wessex Novels in any way equal to the demand among my Red Cross friends (who read infernally fast) and others of the elect; nor did the two complete Kipling sets, ordered long before the library was opened, ever look like coming. These authors we had only in odd volumes, and few were the nights they spent upon their shelves. But a novel-reader is a novel-reader, one can generally find him something; my difficulty was in coping with another type altogether—the real bookworm—who is far more particular about his food. Anything but novels for this gentleman as I knew him at the front; and he was often the last person one would have suspected of his particular tastes, sometimes a very young gentleman indeed. There was one such, a rugged lad with a strong Lancashire or Yorkshire accent, whom I thought I should never suit. Lamb, Emerson, Ruskin and Carlyle, he demanded in turn as glibly as Woodbines or Gold Flakes; but either I had them not, or they were out. Macaulay's Essays happened to be in. 'The literary ones?' said the boy, suspiciously, to my suggestion. 'I don't want the political!' I remember he took a Golden Treasury in the end; as already noted, I had several copies, and needed every one.

Then I found that I required a better selection of technical works of all sorts. Engineers, especially, want engineering books and journals; it is a rest to the fighting man to pursue his peace-time interests or studies at the front. Nothing, one can well imagine, takes him out of khaki quicker; and that is what his books are for, nor will he shut them a worse soldier. Of devotional works, as I may have hinted, we opened with a fair number; this was increased later by a strong consignment from Tottenham Court Road. But it was impossible to be too strong on that side—with a Division of Jocks in the sector!

'It's the only subject that interests me,' said a tight-lipped Scottish Rifleman, quite simply, on the third day. He was not a man I would have surrendered to with much confidence on a dark night, but he had brought back a book called The Fact of Christ, and he wanted something else in the same category. Just then there was nothing; but with imbecile temerity I did say we had a number of 'religious novels' by a lady of great eminence. 'I'm no a believer in her,' was his only reply. I can still see his grim ghost of a smile. Himmel help the Hun who sees it first!

The young man vanished for his sixteen days, and in his absence came the bale of theology from Tottenham Court Road.

'Now I've got something for you,' said I when I saw his keen face again; and lifted off its shelf Dr. Norman Macleod's most weighty tome. I cannot check the Parisian typist who rendered the title Caraid nan Gaidherl; the subject, however, was the only one that interested the Scottish Rifleman, and I took the tongue for his very own. My mistake!

'But that'll be in Gaelic,' said he, without opening the book. 'I have never studied Gaelic, though a Highlander born. Now, had it been Hebrew,' and he really smiled, 'I micht have managed!'

I saw he might; for obviously he had been a theological student when he felt it incumbent upon him (especially as such) to play a Jock's part in the Holy War. I saw, too, that his smile was shy and gentle in its depths, only grim on top. I think, after all, he would have given his last cigarette to a prisoner of anything like his own manhood.

But there was one worse failure than any deficiency on our shelves, and that, alas! was my own poor dear New Book Table. I had not looked after it as I ought, and neither had my friend and fellow-worker; in my eagerness to keep our respective departments ideally distinct, this fancy one had fallen between two stools. Several of the new books were missing before we actually missed one; then we took nightly stock, and with mortifying results. At last it could go on no longer, and the new books were replaced by old bound volumes of magazines, more difficult to deport. But I was determined to have it out with the hut; and I chose the next Sunday evening service, in the course of which I made it a rule to have my say about things in general, for the delicate duty.

I didn't a bit like doing it, as I held my regular readers above suspicion, and they formed the bulk of the little congregation; and that night I was in any case more nervous than I meant them to see, as for once I had decided to tackle the 'sermon' myself. It was the first evening of Summer Time; lamplight was unnecessary; and the splendid men sitting at ease in the arm-chairs, which they had drawn up to the platform end, or at the tables or on the floor, made a great picture in the soft warm dusk. One candle glimmered at the piano, and one on that egregious rostrum, as I stood up behind it and trembled in my boots.

I told them the New Book Table had ceased to exist as such; that I had prostrated myself before fifteen of my natural enemies, in order to spread that table to their liking; but that there had been so many desertions from my crack corps that we were obliged to disband it. Not quite so pat as all that, but in some such words (and to my profound relief) I managed to get a laugh, which enabled me to say I thought it hard luck on the ninety-and-nine just persons that the hundredth man should borrow books without going through the preliminary formalities. But I added that if they came across any of the deserters, and would induce them to return to their unit, I should be greatly obliged. They were jolly enough to clap before I launched into my discourse, and it was what their rum ration must have been to them. I wish as much could be done for poor deacons before going over their top.

But the point is that at least one deserter did return next day; and what touched me more, the little gifts of books, which they had taken to bringing me for the library, increased and multiplied from that night. Nor must I forget the humorist (not one of my high-brows) who button-holed me on my way back to the counter:—

'Beg yer pardon, Mr. 'Ornung, but that pinchin' them new books—wasn't a Raffles trick, was it?'

But if we failed where I had thought we were doing something extra clever, we met with great success in a less deliberate innovation for which I can claim but little credit.

In our quiet hut there was no need for the usual Quiet Room; but there it was, at the platform end, as much use as in the heart of the Great Sahara. I had thought of turning it into a little informal sort of lecture-room, for readings and other entertainments which might not be to everybody's taste. But I had no time to organise or run a side-show; neither of us had a spare moment in the beginning. Though we never opened in the morning, except to officers who cared to come in as friends, there was plenty to do behind the scenes—parcels of new books to unpack and acknowledge, supplementary catalogues to prepare—all manner of preparations and improvements that took the two of us all our time. Then my second mate, the minister, fell from Heaven—for he was just our man.

He had made a hobby of the literary evening in his Border parish; had come out armed with a number of vivacious appreciations of his favourite authors, the very thing for our Quiet Room. I handed it over to him forthwith, and we embarked together upon a series of Quiet Room Evenings, which I do believe were a joy to all concerned. At any rate we always had an audience of forty or fifty enthusiasts, who took part in the closing discussion, and in time might have been encouraged to put up a better lecture than either of us. The minister, however, was very good; and what he had cut out, in his unselfish pursuit of brevity, I could sometimes put into a more ponderous performance at the end. It was a greater chance than any that one got on Sunday evening; for though I promise them there was never any previous idea of improving the occasion, yet it was impossible to sit, pipe in mouth, chatting about some great writer to that roomful of thinking, fighting men, and not to touch great issues unawares. Life and death—wine and women—I almost shudder to think what subjects were upon us before we knew where we were! But a great, big, heavenly heart beat back at me, the composite heart of fifty noblemen on easy terms with Death; and if they heard anything worth remembering, it came from themselves as much as though they had written the things down and handed them up to me to read out. I have known an audience of young schoolboys as kindlingly responsive to a man who loved them; but here were grown soldiers on the battle's brink; and their high company, and their dear attention, what a pride and privilege were they!

If only it had been earlier in the season, not the very hush before the hurricane! There were so many lives and works that we were going to thresh out together—Francis Thompson's, for one. He had crept into our evening with Edgar Allan Poe. I had promised them a long evening with Francis; the stretcher-bearers, especially, were looking forward to it as much as I was; but I had to send for the books, and they were not in time.

And on the last of these Quiet Room Evenings, a young lad in a Line regiment had stayed behind and said:

'May we have a lecture on Sir John Ruskin, sir?'

I said of course they might—but I was not competent to deliver it myself. His books were on the way, however, for there had been more than one inquiry for them. They also arrived too late.

I had never seen the boy before, nor did I again. I may this winter. He shall have his 'lecture on Sir John Ruskin'—if I have to get it up myself!

WRITERS AND READERS

For my own ends I kept a kind of librarian's ledger, in which was entered, under the author's name, every book that ever went out, together with its successive dates of departure and return. This amateurish scheme may not have been worth the labour it entailed, in spare moments at the counter or last thing at night, after a turn-over of perhaps a hundred volumes, many of which needed new labels before retiring to the shelf. But I was never sorry I had let myself in for it. Theoretically, one had only to look up a book in this ledger to tell whether it was in or out; but in practice my reward was not then, but is now, when I can see at a glance who really were our popular authors, and which books of theirs were never without a partner, and which proved wall-flowers.

Statistics, however, are notoriously bad witnesses; and some of mine would not stand cross-examination. Thus, take him for all in all, the author of The First Hundred Thousand may add the blue ribbon of the Rest Hut to his collection; but then, we had practically all his books, and some of them four or five deep. Nor was the one that had more outings than anything of anybody's on our shelves on that account the most popular; it may even have been the author's nearest approach to a bad penny. On the other hand, our four copies of The First Hundred Thousand were out almost as long as we were open, and all four 'failed to return.' As for its sequel, our only copy eloped with its first partner: had all our authors been Ian Hays there would have been no carrying on the library after the first hundred thousand seconds.

The run on these two books was the more noteworthy in view of the fighting reader's distaste for 'shop.' It was the flattering exception to a very human rule; for I find, taking a good many days at random, that while all but thirteen of every hundred issues were novels, less than three of the thirteen were books about the war. Some forty-nine readers out of fifty wanted something that would take them out of khaki, and nearly nine out of ten pinned their faith to fiction.

How many preferred a really good novel is another and a more invidious matter; but nothing was more refreshing than the way the older masters held their own. Dickens was in constant demand, especially among the older men; and they really read him, judging by the days the immortal works stayed out. Again, it was worth noting that here in France A Tale of Two Cities had twice as many readers as Pickwick, which came next in order of popularity. Thackeray was not fully represented, but we had all his best and they were always out. Of the Brontës we had next to nothing, of Reade and Trollope far too little; but It is Never too Late to Mend enchanted a Sapper, a Machine Gunner, and a Red Cross man in turn, while Orley Farm would have headed our first day's list had it been there in time. George Eliot was never without readers, but Miss Braddon had more, and The Woman in White only one! After Dickens, however, the most popular Victorian was the first Lord Lytton.

I confess it rejoiced my heart to hand out the protagonists of a belittled age at least as freely as their 'opposite numbers' of the present century. But I had my surprises. Scott (Sir Walter!) was a firm wall-flower for the first fortnight; probably the Jocks knew him off by heart; and, of course, the same thing may apply to their unnatural neglect of the so-called Kaleyard School of other days. There was, at any rate, nothing clannish about their reading. It was a Jock who took The Unspeakable Scot for its only airing; and more than three-fourths of my Stevensonians were Sassenachs. But one could still conjure with the name of Stevenson, as with many another made in his time. Mr. Kipling's soldiers are adored by legions created in their image. Sir H. Rider Haggard was never on the Rest House shelf. Messrs. Holmes and Watson were the most flourishing of old firms, and Gerard the only Brigadier taken seriously at my counter. Ruritania, too, got back some of its own trippers from the Five Towns; for though you would have thought there was adventure enough in the air we breathed, there was more realism, and it was against the realism we all reacted. Mr. Bennett, to be sure, did not occupy nearly enough space in our capricious catalogue; neither, for that matter, did Mr. Weyman, Mr. Galsworthy, Mr. Vachell, nor yet Miss Marie Corelli or Sir Thomas Hall Caine. The fault was not mine, I can assure them.

Mr. H. G. Wells, on the other hand, utilised a better chance by tying with the author of Arsène Lupin, and just beating Mr. Phillips Oppenheim, for a place it would be unprofitable to compute. Even they could not live the pace of Mr. Charles Garvice, who in his turn succumbed to the lady styled the Baroness Horsy by her fondest slaves; to these two and to Miss Ethel Dell, among others I have or have not presumed to mention, I could wish no greater joy than my job at that counter when their books were coming in, and 'another by the same author, if you've got one,' being urgently demanded in their place. The most enthusiastic letter ever written for an autograph could not touch the eager tone, the live eye, the parted lips of those unconscious tributes. It is not the look you see in Mudie's as you wait your turn; but I have seen it in small boys chasing pirates with 'Ballantyne the Brave,' and in one old lady who fell in love every Sunday of her dear life with the hero of The Family Herald Supplement. It was even better worth seeing in a soldier with Just a Girl in his ruthless hand, and The One Girl in the World trembling on a reverential tongue. The man might have been performing prodigies of dreadful valour up the Line, but his soul had been on leave with a lady in marble halls.

There were two young Privates in the A.S.C. who bolted their Garvice at about two days to the book; and two trim Corporals of the Rifle Brigade who made as short work of the other magicians. This type of reader always hunted in couples, sharing the most sympathetic of all the passions, if not the books themselves, which would double the rate of consumption. They were the hard drinkers at my bar; but the hardest of all was a lean young Jock, who smiled as hungrily as Cassius, and arrived punctually at six every evening to change his book. He looked delicate, and was, I think, like other regular attendants, on light duty in the town; in any case he took his bottle of fiction a day without fail, and once, when it was raining, drained it under my nose and wanted another. I refused to serve him. Unlike the other topers, he was a sardonic critic. One night he banged the counter with a book in my own old line, and the invidious comment:

'He can do what you no can!'

I said I was sure, but inquired the special point of superiority.

'He can kill his mon as often as he likes,' said McCassius, grimly, 'and bring him to life again. Fufty times he has killed yon mon—fufty times!'

They were very nice to me about my books—but very honest! There was a certain stretcher-bearer, a homely old fellow with a horse-shoe moustache and mild brown eyes; not from the high-brow unit, but perhaps a greater reader than any of them; and one of those who eschewed the novel. Scenes of Clerical Life (on top of Lenotre's Incidents of the French Revolution, and our two little volumes of Elia) had been his only dissipation until, our friendship ripening, he weighed me with his tranquil eyes and asked for Raffles. I seemed to detect a streak of filial piety in the departure, and gave him as fair warning as I could; but only the book itself could put him off. He returned it without a word to temper his forgiving smile, and took out The Golden Treasury as a restorative. Poetry he loved with all his gentle soul; but when, at a later stage, he asked if I thought he could 'learn to write poetry,' the wounds of vanity were at least anointed.

He used to take down Mr. David Somervell's capital Companion to the Golden Treasury from the Poetry Shelf; and it was delightful to watch his bent head wagging between text and note, a black-rimmed forefinger creeping down either page, and his back as round as it could possibly have been before the war. He told me he was a Northamptonshire shoemaker by trade; and though you would trust him not to scamp a sole or bump a stretcher, there was nothing to show that the war meant more to him than his last, or life more than a chance of reading—the shadow lengthening in the sunshine that he found in books. Once I said how I envied him all that he had read; very gently—even for him—he answered that he owed it all to his mother, who had taught him when he was so high, and would be eighty-one come Tuesday. The man himself was only forty; but he was one of those guileless creatures who make one unconsciously look up to them as elders as well as betters. And at the front, where the old are so gloriously young, and the young so pathetically old, nothing is easier than to forget one's own age: often enough mine was brought home to me with a salutary shock.

'When I was up the Line,' said one of my friends, bubbling over with a compliment, 'a chap said to me, "You know that old—that—that elderly man who runs the Rest Hut? He's the author of Raffles!"'

Disastrous refinement! And the fellow grinned as though he had not turned what might have been a term of friendship into one of pure opprobrium. Elderly! One would as lief be labelled Virtuous or Discreet.

Another of my poetry lovers did really write it—but not his own—there was too much of a twinkle in his brown eyes! They were twinkling tremendously when I saw them first, fixed upon the Poetry Shelf, and the tightest upper lip in the hut seemed to be keeping down a cheer. No sooner had we spoken than he was saying he kept his own anthology in his field pocket-book—and could I remember the third verse of 'Out of the night that covers me'? Happily I could; and so made friends with a man after my heart of hearts.

In the first place, he spoke the adorable accent of my native heath or thereabouts; and the things he said were as good as the way he said them. Sense and sensibility, fun and feeling, candour and reserve, all were there in perfect partnership, and his twinkling eyes lit each in turn. Before the war he had been a postal telegraphist, and 'there wasn't a greater pacifist alive'; now he was an R.E. signaller attached to the Guards, and as for pacifism—the twinkle sharpened to a glitter and his upper lip disappeared.

Yet another man of forty, he had joined up early, and assigned any credit to his wife—'good lass!' He was splendid about her and their cheery life together; there was a happy marriage, if you like! 'Ever a rover,' as he said romantically (but with the twinkle), he might be in a post-office, but his heart was not; and it seemed the couple were one spirit. Every summer they had taken their holiday tramping the moors, their poets in their pack: 'when we were tired we would sit down and read aloud.' No wonder the Poetry Shelf made him twinkle! There were two cheery children, 'shaping' as you would expect; their dad borrowed my If to copy out for the small boy's birthday, as well as in his field anthology.

Loyalty to one's own, when so impassioned, is by way of draining the plain man's stock: perfect home lives are not so common that the ordinary middle-aged ratepayer makes haste to give up one for the wars. But the anthologist had not been 'wrapped up' like the rest of us. His loyalties did not even end at his country. That first afternoon, I remember, he told me he had been 'a bit of a Theosophist.'

'Aren't you one now?'

'No; but I still have a warm corner in my heart for them.'

I thought that very finely said of a creed outlived. Give me a warm corner for an old love, be it man, woman, or sect!

Daily he dropped in to read and chat; not to take out a book until his turn came for the Line. It was just when the German push seemed imminent to many, was indeed widely expected at a date when my friend would still be at his dangerous post. He knew well what it might mean at any moment; and I think he said, 'The wireless man must be the last to budge,' with the smile he kept for the things he meant; but for once his eyes were not doing their part. 'Well, thank God I've had it!' he said of his happy past as we locked hands. 'And nothing can take it away from you,' I had the nerve to say; for these may be the comforts of one's own heart, but it seems an insolence to offer them to a younger man with a harder grip on life. Happily we understood each other. 'And many happy chats had we,' he had written on the back of the photograph he left me. He had also written his wife's address. David Copperfield went with him when we parted. I wondered if I should ever see either of them again.

Sure enough, on the predicted night, came the roll of drum-fire, as like thunder as a noise can be; but it was our drum-fire, as it happened, and down came my friend next day to tell me all about it. No-Man's Land had been 'boiling like cocoa' under our shells; he was full of the set-back administered to Jerry, of the fun of underground wireless and the genius of Charles Dickens. I sent him back with Joseph Vance, and we talked of nothing else at our next meeting. It was our last; but I treasure a letter (telling of 'the ruined city of our friendship,' among other things), and a field-card of more recent date; and have every hope that the writer is still lighting up underground danger-posts with his wise twinkle, and still adding to his field anthology.

Yet another hard reader was a Coldstream Guardsman, a much younger man, and one of the handsomest in the hut. He, too, if you will believe me, had brown eyes—a thing that could not happen to three successive characters in a novel—but of another order altogether. If they had never killed a lady in their time, their molten glow belied them. This young man liked a classic author of full flavour. Tom Jones was probably his favourite novel, but we had it not. De Maupassant would have enchanted him— but not the coarse translations on vile paper—or Rousseau's or Cellini's open secrets. As it was he had to put up with Anatole France, and oddments of Swift and Wilde; nor do I forget his justifiable disgust on discovering too late that our Gulliver was a nursery version. He was a delightful companion across the counter: subtle, understanding, soft-spoken, in himself a romantic figure, yet engagingly vulnerable to romance.

'I'm feeling sentimental, Mr. Hornung. I want a love-story,' he sighed one afternoon. I reminded him that he would also want Good Stuff, and succeeded in meeting all his needs with Ships that Pass in the Night.

Next day we had our Quiet Room Evening with Tom Hood; and that was the time I strayed upon delicate ground by way of 'The Bridge of Sighs,' from poem to subject before I knew where I was. The men took it beautifully, and touched my heart by impulsively applauding the very things I should have feared to say to them upon reflection. As for our Coldstreamer, he came straight up to the counter and took out Jeremy Taylor's Holy Living and Dying!

WAR AND THE MAN

Not a day but some winning thing was said or done by one or other of them. A man whom I hardly knew had been changing his book when he heard me talking about green envelopes.

'Do you want a green envelope?' he asked point-blank.

'As a matter of fact, I do.'

'Then I'll see if I can't get you one.'

Now, the point about the 'green envelope' is the printed declaration on the outside, that the contents 'refer to nothing but private and family matters'; this being signed by the sender, your letter is censorable only at the base, and will not be read by anybody with whom you are in daily contact. There is, I believe, a weekly issue of one of these envelopes per man. This I only remembered as the generous soul was turning away.

'Don't you go giving me anything you want yourself!' I called after him.

He just looked over his shoulder. 'Then it wouldn't be much of a gift, would it?' was all he said; but I shall never give a copper to a crossing-sweeper without trying to forget his words.

That man was a driver in the R.H.A., and beyond the fact that he had just been reading The White Company I know nothing about him. They cropped up under every cap-badge, these crisp, articulate, enlightening men; they had shaken off their marching feet the dust of every walk in civil life, and it was only here and there a tenacious speck caught the eye. I have heard a Southern in Jock's clothing work in a word about the season-ticket and the 'silk hat' of his City days; but as a rule a soldier no more thinks of trading upon his civilian past than a small boy at a Public School dreams of bragging about his people. More than in any community on earth, the man at the front has to depend upon his own personality, absolutely without any extraneous aid whatsoever; and the knowledge that he has to do so is a tremendous sharpener of individuality.

Yet your arrant individualist is the last to see it. I remember recommending The Private Papers of Henry Ryecroft to a young man full of brains and sensibility—one of that Field Ambulance to which, as we saw it, the description applies in bulk. He came back enthusiastic, as I knew he would, and we discussed the book. I quarrelled with the passage in which Gissing rails at the weekly drill in his school playground: 'even after forty years' the memory brought on a 'tremor of passionate misery.... The loss of individuality seemed to me sheer disgrace.' My Red Cross friend applauded the sentiments that I deplored; himself as individual as a man need be, he assured me that the Army did crush the individuality out of a man; and when, refraining from the argumentum ad hominem, I called his attention to many others present who showed no sign of such subdual, he said at any rate it happened to the weaker men.

It may: and if a man has no personality of his own, will he be so much the worse for the composite substitute to be acquired in the Army? Better an efficient machine than a mere nonentity; but an efficient machine may be many things besides, and, under the British system, nearly always is. The truth is that discipline and restriction do not 'crush' the normal personality in the least. They compress it; and compression is strength. They prevent a man from 'slopping over'; they conserve his essence. They may not 'make a man' of one who is a man already, but they do exalt and intensify the quality of manhood; they do make a good man in that sense better, and a goodish man out of many a one who has been accounted 'no good' all his life.

Often when the hut was full of magnificent young life; bodies at their very best, perfect instruments in perfect tune; minds inquisitive, receptive, experienced beyond the dreams of pre-war philosophy, and honest as minds must be on the brink of Beyond; often and often have I looked down the hut and compared the splendid fellows I saw before me with the peace-time types perceptibly represented by so many. Small tradesmen, clerks, shop assistants, grooms and gardeners, labourers in every overcrowded field, what they were losing in the softer influences of life, that one might guess, but what they were gaining all the time, in mind, body, and character, that one could see. It did not lessen the heart-break of the thought that perhaps half would never see their homes again; but it did console with the conviction that the half who survived would be twice the men they ever would or could have been without the war. Nay, they were twice their old selves already, if I am any judge of a man who talks to me. I only know I never foregathered with a couple of them without feeling that we were all three the harder and yet the tenderer men for our humble sacrifices, our aching hearts and our precarious lives. I never looked thoughtfully upon a body of these younger brothers without thinking of the race to spring from loins so tried in such a fire. Never—if only because it was the first comfort that came to mind.

But it was not the only one. Here before my eyes, day after day, were scores of young men not only 'in the pink,' but in better 'form' than perhaps they themselves suspected; not only intensely alive but manifestly enjoying life, the corporate life of constant comradeship and a common if sub-conscious excitement, to an extent impossible for them to appreciate at the time. They put me in mind of a man I know who volunteered for South Africa in his athletic youth, and has ever since been celebrated among his friends for the remark of a lifetime. Somebody had asked him how he liked the Army. 'The Army?' cried this young patriot. 'Once a soldier, always a civilian!' None the less, he was one of those I met in France, a Major in the A.S.C., which he had joined (under a false age) at the beginning of the war. And how many, now the first to adopt his watchword, would not jump at the chance to emulate his deed in another fifteen unadventurous years!

Many, we are told, will anticipate the inconceivable by making their own adventures, if not their own war on society, such are the brutalising effects of war! In this proposition there is probably as much as a grain of truth to a sandhill of imbecility; but we shall hear of that grain on all sides; the soldier-criminal will be only too certain of a copious press, the bombing burglar of his headline. The people we are not going to hear about, and have no desire to recognise as such, are the rascals reformed, the weak men strengthened, the prodigals born again in this war, and at least less likely to die a second death-in-life. With all my heart I believe that, with few exceptions, the only characters which will have suffered by the war are those of such youngish men as have managed to stand out of it to the end, and men of all ages and all conditions who have failed throughout to put their personal considerations in their pockets, and left it to other men and other men's sons to die or bleed for them. I hope they are not more numerous than the men who have been 'brutalised' by war. At all events there were no successful shirkers about our huts in France; and that may have made the atmosphere what it was. All might not have the heart for war; here and there some sapient head might wag aloof; but at least all had their lives and bodies in the cause, there were no safe skins, no cold detachment, no complacent lookers-on. It was an atmosphere of manhood the more potent for the plain fact that no man regarded himself as such in any marked degree, or for one moment in the light of a hero.

That is all I have to say about their heroism. It is an absolute, like the beauty of Venus or the goodness of God. Daily and hourly they are rising to heights that keep all the world always wondering—when, indeed, it does not kill the power of wonderment. But their dead level, the level on which I saw them every day, lies high enough for me. It is not only what discipline has done for them, not only what the habit of sacrifice has made of them, that appeals and must appeal to the older man privileged to mix with soldiers at the front. It is also the wonderful quality of his fellow-countrymen as revealed in these tremendous years. That was there all the time, but it took the war to show it up, it took the war to make us see it. I might have known that rough poor lads were reading Ruskin and Carlyle, that a Northamptonshire shoemaker was as likely as anybody else to be steeped in Charles Lamb, or a telegraph-clerk and his wife to tramp the Yorkshire dales with Wordsworth and Keats about their persons. Yet I, for one, more shame for me! would never have imagined such men if the God of battles had not put me to school in my Rest Hut for one short half-term.

Neither could I have invented, at my best or worst, a young City clerk who played the piano divinely by the hour together, or a very shy young man, a chemist's assistant from the most unhallowed suburb, for whom I had to order Beethoven and Chopin, Liszt and Brahms and Schumann, because he could play even better, but not from memory. Those two lads were the joy of the hut, of hundreds who frequented it. And how much joy had they given in their lodgings or behind the shop? Who had ever been prouder of them than their comrades, or done so much to 'bring them out'? Yet, need I say it? they both belonged to that clever, intellectual, fascinating Field Ambulance to which the Rest Hut owed so much; and I shouldn't wonder if they both agreed with that other nice fellow, their thoroughly individual comrade who declared that 'the Army crushes the individuality out of a man!'

'WE FALL TO RISE'

BEFORE THE STORM

That dramatic month would have been memorable for the weather if for nothing else. Day after day 'the March sun felt like May,' if ever it did; and though it dried no hawthorn-spray in the broken heart of our little old town, and there was neither blade nor petal to watch a-blowing and a-growing, yet Spring was in our nostrils and we savoured it the more eagerly for all we knew it must bring forth. Then the overshadowing ruins took on glorious hues in the keen sunlight, especially towards evening; the outer grey so warm and soft, like a mouse's fur; the inner lining, of aged brick, an even softer tone of its own, neither red nor pink. Day after day a clean sky threw the jagged peaks into violent relief, and high lights snowed their Matterhorn, until a sidelong sunset picked the whole chain out with shadows like falls of ink. It was a sin to spend those afternoons indoors, even in the Rest Hut, where the two stoves stood idle for days on end, and all the windows open.

Then there were the still and starry nights. Then there were the moonlight nights, not so still, but nothing very dreadful happening our way. Our big local gun might have gone on tour; at least I seem to remember many a night when it did not shake us in our beds, when indeed there was little but the want of sheets and pillow-cases to remind us that we were not in England, where after all one can hear more guns than are noticed any longer, and an aeroplane at any hour of the twenty-four. Many a night there was no more than that to remind us that we were only just behind the Line.

Sometimes, as the two of us sat last thing over a nice open fireplace that had found its way into my room from one of the skeleton houses on the opposite side of the square, one or other would fall to moralising upon the past life of the place we had made so much our own. It was a dutiful effort to remember that the Hôtel de Ville had not always been a mangled pile, its palisaded courtyard once something other than the site of a Y.M.C.A. hut. But the reflection failed to haunt us as it might have done; the present and the living were too absorbing, to say nothing of the imminent future; and as for the dead past, we had our own. And yet we knew from guide-book and album what shining pools of parquet, what ceilings heavily ornate, what monumental intricacies in wood and stone, what crystal grandiosities, formed the huge rubbish-heaps between the mouse-grey walls with the reddish lining: we knew, but it was no use trying to care. The Hôtel de Ville had finished its course; the Rest Hut was just getting into its stride. Another chunk off the stump of the once delicate and dizzy belfry, what did it signify unless the chunk came through our roof? That was our only anxiety in the matter, and we debated whether such a chunk would fly so far, or fall straight down as apparently the rest of the campanile had done before it. My chief mate, however, wound up every debate with the reiterated conviction that there would be no German push at all; they were 'not such fools' as to make one. But for my part I never went to bed without wondering whether that would be the last of our quiet nights, or a quiet night at all. And deadly quiet they had grown; even the rats no longer disturbed us; every one of them had departed, and for no adequate reason within our knowledge. Even the sceptic of a mate had something trite but sinister to say about 'a sinking ship.' ...

One afternoon, two days before the date on which most people seemed to expect things to happen, a harbinger arrived as I sat perched behind the counter. We were not long open; most of the men present were clustered round the newspaper table; you really could have heard some pins drop. That was why, for a second or two, I did hear something I had never heard before, and have no wish to hear again. It sounded exactly like a miniature aeroplane approaching at phenomenal speed. I was just beginning to wonder what it was when there followed the most extraordinary crash. Not an explosion; not a breakage; but the loud flat smack a dining-table might make if you hauled it up to a ceiling by its castors and let it fall perfectly evenly upon a bare floor. It was the roof, however, that had been hit.

We went out to look, and one of the men picked up a fragment of shell, only about three inches long and less than an inch wide. That was my table-top. The jagged edge of it glittered as though incrusted with tiny brilliants; but the fragment was quite cold, showing that it had travelled far since the burst. 'One of our Archies,' said most of the men; but the Rest Hut orderly, who wore a Gunner badge said laconically: 'Fritz—range-finding!' He was borne out by a High Commander who honoured me with a visit some days later. I believe it was the first bit of German stuff that had found its way into the middle of the town since the previous November; and a very interesting and effective little entry it made, in the quietest hour of one of those uncannily quiet days, and in the precincts of what we flattered ourselves was the quietest hut on any front. But the funny (and rather disappointing) thing was that it had failed to leave so much as its mark upon our roof. It must have skimmed the apex and glanced off the downward slope—convex side down—as a stone glances off a pond. 'The little less,' and it would have drilled the reverse slope like a piece of paper. I have often thought of that cluster of forage caps, under the silky skylights, round the central table; but what I shall always hear, plainer than the terrific smack that left no mark, is that first little singing whirr as of a dwarf propeller of gigantic power. I think that must be the most sickening sound of all under heavy shell-fire in the open.

Next day was the eve of the expected attack, which did not in point of fact take place for another week and more; but how widespread was the expectation we learnt for ourselves by our own small signs and portents. A dozen francs were refunded on a dozen books whose borrowers were afraid they would have no more time just then to read another; but when it all blew over for that week, back they came with their deposits, and out went more books than ever. The mate was jubilant. Of course there had been no German attack; and never would be; they were not such fools! Nor was he by any means alone in his opinion; many officers—but enough! We were not, to be sure, by way of meeting many officers. And yet Wednesday, March 20th, brought two to my room whose respective deliverances are worth remembering in the light of subsequent events.

One was the Gunner who had given me steak and onions on our All Uppingham day in the dark depths of the earth. He was as cheery as if he had been making another century in the Old Boys' Match, instead of having just gone on with his heavies on a new pitch altogether. It was going to suit him. He felt like getting wickets. And the Pavilion was not a dug-out this time; it was an elephant, in which the Major and he could put me up any night I liked. Why not that night? He had come in a car; he could take me back with him.

Why not, I sometimes wonder to this day! There were good, there were even creditable, reasons; but, beyond the fact that I was now much attached to my counter, I honestly forget what they were. I only know that my hospitable friend's new wicket was one of the first to be overrun by a field-grey mob; and though the Major and he are still enjoying rude health on the right side of the Line, and it goes without saying that they left the ground with becoming dignity, I am afraid I should have been out of place in the procession. Exciting moments I must have had, but I should have been sorry to play Anchises to my friend's Æneas. And I was to have my little moments as it was.

My other visitor was, curiously, another cricketer, whom I had first seen bowling in the University match at Lord's. It is not his department of the greater game; nor do I intend to compromise this officer by means of any further clue; for he it was who informed me that the push was really coming before morning. 'So they say,' he smiled, and we passed on to matters of more immediate interest. Time enough to be interested in the push when it did come; from all reports I was likely to find myself in the stalls, and he of course would be on the stage. So that was that. In the meantime I had a great fixture arranged and billed for the Saturday evening. An old friend was coming over from the Press Château to lecture in the Rest Hut, for the first time on any platform; there were to be seats for all our other friends, officers and men, and some supper in my room for half-a-dozen of us and the lecturer. It was of this we talked, and probably of pre-war cricket, and my beloved men, over the last quiet tea I was to have there. Books went out very freely till we closed. With Our Faces to the Light, Heroes and Hero-Worship, The Supreme Test, and Our Life after Death, were among the last half-dozen titles!

ANOTHER OPENING DAY

... It did not wake me up till four or five in the morning. Then I knew it had begun. The row was incessant rather than tremendous; not nearer than it had often been, when that big local gun was at home, but indubitably different. Some supplementary sound followed most of the reports, as the receding swish of a shattered breaker follows the first crash. I guessed what it was, but I wanted to be sure. I wanted to ask the mate, on the other side of the partition behind my head; but I didn't want to wake him up on purpose. The only unnerved man I met in France, one of our workers whose railway-carriage had been blown in by a bomb on the last stage of his journey from the coast, had awakened the man in the next bed for company's sake the night after. He was brave enough to own it. I wanted company, but I had not the hardihood to sing out for it until I heard a movement through the partition.

The mate, of course, did not believe it was the push; but he confessed it sounded the sort of thing one would expect to hear if the Germans were fools enough to make a push. It sounded like rather distant thunder, with sporadic claps in the middle distance. I smoked a pipe with my Spectator before trying for some more sleep, and was just dropping off when our orderly arrived with jaunty tread.

'It's Fritz,' said he, with sardonic unconcern. 'You can hear the houses coming down.'

And there followed the tale of damage done so far.

I am afraid we were both up with the wind, if not with the sun. But we shaved without bloodshed; for it is remarkable how a shell-burst can fail to jog your elbow, or to spill your tea, when you have been educated up to that type of disturbance. We had grown so used to guns in the night that the quiet nights were the uncanny ones; and even they were generally punctuated first or last by a comfortable bang from the local heavy; the 'All's Well!' of that night-watchman, which, if it woke us up, only encouraged us to go to sleep again with an increased sense of security. A shell-burst at a decent distance sounded much the same for the first—and only startling—second. And all that morning, and generally throughout the day, they kept their distance with quite unexpected decency.

But they did sing over our heads; they did keep the blue above us vocal with their shrill, whining cries; it was astounding to look up into the unruffled heavens and see no trace of their course. As one gazed, the crash came in the streets a few hundred yards away; and often after the crash, by an interval of seconds, a noise as of some huge cart shooting its rubbish. Somebody said it was like a great lash whistling over us and cracking amid the herd of living houses just beyond. It really was; and what followed was the groan as yet another piece was taken out of the palpitating town.

Two things came home to us while the day was young. It was biggish stuff that was coming in, at a longish range; and it was coming in on business, not on pleasure. Its business was to feel for barracks, batteries, and other sound investments for valuable munitions; not to have a sporting flutter here, there, and everywhere; much less to indulge in the sheer luxury of pestling a ruined area to powder. If or when they made some ground, and brought up their field-guns, it would be a different matter; then it might pay them to keep us skipping in all parts of the town at once; but, for the present, we in our part were in quite ignoble security—unless Fritz lost his strength! We had, however, to remember that we were in a straight line between wicket and wicket; nor did his singing deliveries give us much chance of forgetting the fact.

News was not long in reaching us from less fortunate localities. The station was catching it; and we had a busy hut all but adjoining the station. We looked upon our comrades at the Station Hut with mingled envy and commiseration, when one or two of them dropped in to recount their adventures and escapes. A short-pitched one had killed four officers in the street in their direction. And it so happened that business took me to the spot during the course of the morning.

It would be idle to pretend it was an enjoyable expedition. A friend went with me; we wore our shrapnel helmets, and everybody we met was wearing his. That alone gave the streets an altered appearance; otherwise everything wore its normal aspect; the March sun was more like May than ever, the sky more innocently blue, the cool light hand of spring softer and more caressing. On the way we met two chaplains of the Guards, who gave us details of the tragedy; on its scene we saw clean wounds on the stone facing of a house, the chipped places standing out in the strong sunlight, but did not investigate too closely. Two of the officers had been standing in the doorway, two crossing the open space we skirted; two had been killed outright, and two were dying or dead of their wounds. Shells whistled continuously as we walked, but not one burst before our eyes.

On my return the mate and I had a look at a dungeon under the Town Hall, as a possible sleeping-place. It was part of an underground system for which the town was famous. One could walk for miles, from chamber to chamber, as one can crawl from cell to cell in the foundations of most big houses. We had long talked of going to ground there, with all our books, in the day of battle; and now we viewed provisional sites, though only one of us allowed that the day had dawned.

'This is not the push,' I was stoutly assured. 'This is only a feint, man. They are not such fools ...'

After lunch we opened to the bang and whistle of our own guns, for a change. The sacred mid-day meal was never followed up by enemy gun-fire in my hearing; the time-table obviously included a methodical siesta, which it was our daily delight to spoil. Not that my Rest Hut crowd betrayed much pleasure in the proceedings; for once, indeed, I could not help thinking them rather a stolid lot. There they sat as usual under the sunny skylights, dredging the day's news as though it were the one uninteresting thing in the hut, or playing dominoes and draughts, like a nurseryful of unnaturally good children. It is difficult to describe their demeanour. To say that they looked as though nothing was happening is to imply a studied unconcern; and there was certainly nothing studied on their side of the counter; on ours, it seemed as if the Rest Hut had only needed this external din to make it really restful.

'Our friend Jerry's a bit saucy this morning,' said the emissary of a sick Sergeant who sent for a fresh Maurice Hewlett every day that week. It was the first comment of the afternoon on the day's events. 'Our friend Jerry' had risen from his siesta and was giving us whistle and bang for our bang and whistle; and still every shot sounded plumb over the hut. It was like the middle of a tennis-court during a hard rally; but I never heard anybody suggest that either side might hit into the net.

Then, I remember, came a new-comer, a husky lad with a poisoned wrist.

'Gimme one o' them books.'

I had my formula in such cases.

'Who is your favourite author?'

'Don't know as I have one; gimme any good yarn.'

'What's the best yarn you ever read?'

'I don't often read one.'

'The last you did read?'

Lost in the mists. I set The Hound of the Baskervilles on him, and saw him well bitten by the book before the afternoon was out or the bombardment by way of abating. There was no tea-interval on the other side, that I remember; but we had ours as usual in my room, and it was either that afternoon or the next that an eminent Oxford professor, out on a lecturing tour, gave us his company. He was delightfully interested in the library, and spent most of the afternoon behind the counter, making out a list of books he talked of sending us, chatting with the men, and endearing himself to us all. I daresay he was the oldest man who had ever entered the hut; but I still see him perched on top of our little home-made step-ladder, in overcoat and muffler and soft felt hat, while the shells burst nearer, or at any rate made more noise, as the day drew in. Book in hand, and a kindly, interested, quizzical smile upon his face, the professor looked either as though he never heard one of them, or as though he had heard little else all his life. He cheered one more than the cheeriest soldier, for his was not the insensibility of usage, but the selfless preoccupation of a lofty soul.

Earlier in the week I had accepted an invitation to dine that evening with a mess at the other end of the town. It was quite the wrong end for dinner at such a time; it was the end where the German shells were feeling about for things worth smashing. They kept skimming across the streets as I found my way through the dusk, and ours came skimming back; it was the tennis-court again, but this time one seemed to be crossing it on gigantic stilts, head and shoulders above the chimney-pots. But nothing happened. It was a seasoned mess, all padres and doctors, to the best of my recollection; and they gave one a confidence more welcome than all their conscious hospitality. I enjoy my evening immensely—as I look back.

There was a window at each end of the dinner-table. No sooner were we seated than there occurred outside one of these windows about the loudest explosion I ever heard. No chair was pushed back, and I am bound to say that was the end of it; they said it was further off than I can yet believe. They also seemed to think it was a bomb. There I trusted they were right. Bombs cannot go on falling on or even about the same place. But in fifteen minutes to the tick we had the same thing outside the other window. This time the glass came tinkling down, and it was thought worth while to inquire whether there were any casualties in the kitchen. There were none: no doubt some chair would have been pushed back if the answer had been in the affirmative.

And that was all, except a great deal of shell-talk, and comparison of hair-breadth escapes, between my two hosts (both of whom had borne charmed lives—but who has not, out there?) when the rest were gone, and a shower of stuff in the soft soil of the garden as I was going myself. Perhaps 'shower' is too strong a word; but one of the many things I can still hear is the whizz and burial of at least one lethal fragment close beside us in the dark. The kind pair insisted on walking back with me, and were strong in their advice to me to seek a cellar for the night. This being their own intention, and the idea that I found in the mind of my mate on regaining the Rest Hut, he and I spent the next hour in transferring our beds and bedding to the dungeon aforesaid, where I for one slept all the better for the soothing croon of shells high overhead in waking intervals.

It was officially computed that over eight hundred large shells arrived in our little town that day, the historic 21st March, 1918.

THE END OF A BEGINNING

Two capital nights we passed in our ideal dungeon. It was deep yet dry, miraculously free from rats, and so very heavily vaulted, so tucked away under tons of débris, and yet so protected by the standing ruins, that it was really difficult to imagine the projectile that could join the party. There was, to be sure, a precipitous spiral staircase to the upper air, but even it did not descend straight into our lair. Still, a direct hit on the stairs would have been unpleasant; but one ran as much risk of a direct hit by lightning in peace-time. It seems indecent to gloat over a safety verging on the ignoble at such a time; but those two nights it was hard to help it; and the dim morning light upon the warm brick arches, bent like old shoulders under centuries of romance, added an appeal not altogether to the shrinking flesh.

The day between had been very like the first day. I thought the bombardment a shade less violent; but worse news was always coming in. Far fewer books were taken out, far fewer men had their afternoon to themselves, but only too many were their tales of bloodshed, especially on the outskirts of the town. They told them simply, stoically, even with the smile that became men whose turn it might be next; but the smile stopped short at the lips. Still worse hearing was the fall of village after village in sectors all too near our own; and yet more sinister rumours came from the far south. Our greatest anxieties were naturally nearest home, and our chief comfort the unruffled faces of such officers as passed our way. 'He seems to be meeting with some success, too!' as one vouchsafed from his saddle, after an opening in the style of the gentleman who was still demanding Hewletts for his Sergeant.

The second night we had a third cellarman, leader of one of the outlying huts now being abandoned every day. Almost hourly our headquarters were filling up with refugee workers flushed with their sad adventures; but this young fellow had been through more than most; a man had been killed in his hut, and he himself was in the last stages of exhaustion. He had been fast asleep when we descended from the turmoil for our night of peace; and fast asleep I left him in the morning, little thinking that most of us had spent our last night in the neighbourhood.

It was another of those brilliant days we shall remember every March that we may live to see. The devil's choristers were still singing through the blue above, still thundering their own applause in the doomed quarter of the town. Yet to stand blinking in the keen sunlight, snuffing the pure invigorating air, was to vote the whole thing weak and unconvincing. The picturesque ruins were not real ruins. The noises were not the noises of a real bombardment; they were too simple and too innocuous, one had heard them better done upon the stage. It seemed particularly impossible that anything could happen to me, for instance, at the head of my cellar stairs, or to the very immaculate Jocks' Padre picking his way towards me, over a mound of last year's ruins, to us as old as any other hill.

But it was that Padre who struck the sinister note at once. What were we going to do? Do! His meaning was not clear to me; he made it clear without delay. His Jocks—our Jocks—the rocks of my military faith!—had gone away back. Divisional Headquarters, at all events, had shifted out of that; it was the same with the other Divisions in the Corps, the Padre thought; and he took it we should all be ordered back if we didn't go! A place with a ridge had been taken by the enemy, who had only to get his field-guns up—and that was only a question of hours—to make the town a great deal unhealthier than it was already.

I was horrified. It was the one thing I had never contemplated, being turned out of the little old town! After all, it had been an unhealthier spot a year ago than it yet threatened to become again. A year ago the very Line had curled through its narrow rim of suburbs; and yet the troops had stuck to the town; there had been cellarage for all, barricades in streets swept by machine-guns, and a Y.M.C.A. hut run by a valiant veteran through thick and thin. One or two of us, at least, had been prepared for the same thing over again, plus our Rest Cave and all our books at a safe depth underground. That prospect had thrilled and fascinated; the one now foreshadowed seemed too black to come true.

But at breakfast we had it officially from the mere boy (from a Public School, however) in local charge of the lot of us. We had better get packed; it would be safer; but he hoped, perhaps more heartily than any of us, that the extremity in view would not arise. So we pulled out kit-bags and suit-cases of which we had forgotten the sight—and my jolly little room never looked itself again. No room does, once you start packing the belongings that made it what it was; but I never hated that hateful job so much in all my life. Nor did I ever do it worse—which is saying even more. Two days and nights under continuous shell-fire, even when it is only the music of those spheres that he hears incessantly, does find a man out in one way or another. My way was forgetfulness and, I fear, a certain irritability. There are some of my most cherished little possessions that I shall never see again, and a good friend or so with whom I fear I was a trifle gruff. I hope they have forgiven me. But a shell-burst may be easier to bear than a pointless question, especially when you are asking one or two yourself.

At lunch-time the A.P.M. sent in for me. I found him outside in the sun, with the D.A.A. and Q.M.G., I think it was—both of them very grave and business-like in their shrapnel helmets, their gas-masks hooked up under their chins. They, too, wanted to know what we proposed to do; they, too, explained exactly why the town would presently become no place for any of us. But it was not for me to speak for the other workers, who by this time were most of them on the spot; we were all as sheep in the absence of our Public School shepherd, who had gone off in the Ford to seek instructions at Area Headquarters. Some of them, indeed, took the opportunity of speaking for themselves; and who had a better right? It may be only my impression that we all had a good deal to say at the same time: I know I voiced my dream about the Rest Cave. The official faces were not encouraging; indeed, they put their discouragement in words open to an ominous construction. They did not say Janiculum was lost, but they left us perhaps deservedly uneasy on the point.

And it was all idiotically, if not shamefully, exasperating! Those heavy shells still raining into the town; untold pain and damage ensuing every minute; the town-crier with his bell even then upon his rounds, warning civilians to evacuate; little parties of them already under way, here a toothless old lady in her Sunday weeds, a dignified old gentleman pushing a superannuated perambulator full of household gods, a prancing terrier loving the sad excitement of it all; and a man old enough to know better thinking only of his makeshift hut, hardly at all about their lifelong homes compulsorily abandoned in their poor old age, yet with a step so proud and so unfaltering! The perambulator, perhaps, was now a nobler and a sadder treasure than any it contained. But just then the hut was home and treasure-house to me; filled day by day with hearts of gold and souls of iron; and now what would become of it and them!

For the first time since the first day of all, nobody was there when we opened; but presently a handful drifted in, as unconcerned as the terrier in the road, but without a symptom of the dog's ingenuous excitement. What was it to them if the day was big with all our fates! It would not be their first big day; but it was not their day at all just yet, whatever it might be to us. To them it was still a May day come in March, the air was still charged with the fulness of life, and the hut with all that they had found in it hitherto. It was only to us, in our narrow, keen experience, that everything was spoilt, or spoiling before our eyes.

'It's too good a day to waste in war,' said one of them across an idle counter.

It was not his first utterance recorded in these notes; and there seemed a touch of affectation about it. But he was one of the clever lot I liked, and what I thought his self-consciousness only drew us closer; for I defy you to live under shell-fire, for the first time, without thinking of yourself, and what the next moment may mean to you—and what the moment after—at the back of your mind. It is another thing when your hands are full. But the peculiar traffic at our counter had dwindled steadily during the bombardment. And it had lost even more in character than in bulk. Impossible, at least for me, to keep up the tacit pretence that a book was more important than a battle; it had taken our visitor from Oxford (whom I suspect of an eager assent to the proposition) to turn a really deaf ear to the song and crash of high explosive. Mine was hardened, but it heard everything; my mind employed itself on each report; and for the last two days the men and I had been talking War.

But to this young man I talked about his friends whom I might never see again. He had brought back a bundle of their books, and in their names he thanked me for my 'kindness' to them: as if it were all on one side! As if they had not, all of them, done more for me than I for them! They were doing things up to the end; bringing back their books, at their plain inconvenience, on their way to the forefront of the fight; even bringing me, to the eleventh hour, their little offerings of books, the last tokens of their good-will.

It was hard to tell them we were closing down, it might be only for a day or two; harder still to say what one felt without striking an unhelpful note; and I took no risks. We could only refuse their money all the afternoon, entertain them as best we could, and pack them off with a hand-grip and 'Good luck!'

There was trouble, too, behind the scenes. Our dear old Madame was one of those for whom the town-crier had rung a knell; by half-past three she must be out of house, home, and native place. But it was not the shipwreck of her simple life that brought the poor soul in tears to the hut. All the world knows how the homely French take the personal tragedies of war, with the national shrug and a dry eye for their share of the national burden; and Madame was French to her finger-tips. She was therefore an artist, who put her hand to nothing she was not minded to finish as creditably as the good God would let her. Think, then, of her innocent shame at having to deliver our week's laundry wringing wet from the mangle! It was the last mortification; and all our protestations were powerless to assuage the sting to her sensibilities. As for her helpmate, our orderly, for all his capabilities he had never replaced the two heroes of the other hut in my affections; and at this juncture he had managed to get a little drunk. But from information since received one can only wonder it did not happen oftener; for the man had tragedy in his life, and his story would be the most dramatic in these pages had I the heart to tell it. By us he had done more than his duty, and for the hut almost as much as Madame herself. The last sight of each was saddening, and yet a part of the closing scenes, as the pair had been part of our lives.

By half-past five the Y.M.C.A. men had their orders: all to evacuate except four of the youngest or strongest, who might stay for the present to help with the walking wounded. Only too naturally, the Rest Hut was not represented among the chosen. But permission was given us to remain open another hour; and there were perhaps a dozen readers under the still sunny skylights to the end. It went hardest of all to tell them they would have to go. Two or three looked up from the papers to ask in dismay about their lecture. I had forgotten there was to have been a lecture; but here were these children waiting to take their places for the promised treat, and more came later. Nothing all day had illustrated quite so graphically the difference between their point of view and ours; to them bursting shells, falling houses, and emptying town were all in the day's work. They had to carry on just the same; it was more than distasteful to be obliged to point out that we could not. The lecturer, I said, if he was still alive, would be in the thick of things by this time. That went home; he is the man they all read, the man who has sung the praises of the private soldier with an understanding enthusiasm unsurpassed by any war correspondent in any war. A week earlier the hut would have been full to bursting; it shall burst if they like one night this winter—all being better than that Saturday in March—and a war still on!

A regular patron of our Quiet Room Evenings, an oldish man with a fine scorn stamped upon his hard-bitten face, said one or two things I valued the more as coming from him, though I doubt if we had exchanged a dozen words before. I shook his hand, and all their hands, as they went out. They were pleased with us for having kept open a day longer than any of the other huts. I hope I said the other huts had been closed by order; but I only remember wanting to say a great deal more, and thinking better of it. After all, we had understood each other in that hut to a degree beyond the need of heavy speeches.

THE ROAD BACK

There was a strange lull in the firing, and no meal-time to account for it, as I carried the baggage over piecemeal to our headquarters off the opposite end of the little square. The mate was doubtless busy relieving me of my final responsibilities in the matter of stores or accounts; at any rate I remember those two or three halting journeys with his light and my heavy kit. The sun was setting in a slight haze, as though the air were full of gold-dust. The shadows of the crippled houses lay at full length in the square. The big guns were strangely still; their field-guns were taking them a good long time to mount upon the captured ridge. I made my final trip, turned in under the arch at headquarters, where the little Ford 'bus was waiting for the last of us, and incidentally for my last and lightest load. I had not put it in when those infernal field-guns got going.

I do not know what happened in other parts of the town. It seems unlikely that they opened fire on our part in particular, but as I stood talking in a glass passage there came a whirlwind whizz over the low roofs, a crack and a cloud in the adjoining courtyard, and, as I turned back under the arch, another whizz and another bang in the street I had just quitted. So I would have sworn in perfect faith; and for several minutes the street was full of acrid smoke, to bear me out. But it seems the second burst was in the next house, or in the next but one. All I can say is that both occurred within about fifteen paces of the spot where I stood as safe as the house that covered me. And yet the soldiers tell you they prefer shell-fire in the open! With great respect, I shall stick up for the devil I know.

But what has interested me ever since is the hopelessness of expecting two persons to give anything like the same account of a violent experience which has taken them both equally by surprise. Nor is it necessary to go gadding about the front in order to test this particular proposition; try any couple who have been in the same motor accident. It must be done at once, before they have time to compare notes; indeed, they should be kept apart like suspect witnesses in a court. Suspicion will be amply vindicated in nine cases out of ten; for the impression of any accident upon any mind depends on the state of that mind at the time, on the impressions already there, and on its imaginative quality at any time. Hence the totally different versions of the same event from three or four equally truthful persons. A boy I had known all his life was killed just before I went out: three honest witnesses gave three contradictory descriptions of the tragedy. Two of the three were all but eye-witnesses, and C. of E. chaplains at that! No wonder we argued about our beggarly brace of shells. The chief mate (last to leave the ship, by the way) heard three, and a fourth as we drove away in the Ford. My powers of registration were only equal to the two described.

It was good to be high and dry in the little 'bus, though it would have been better with as much as the horn to blow to keep one's mind out of mischief. Our driver was a fine man wearing the South African and 1914 ribbons. Invalided out, he had wormed his way back to France in the Y.M.C.A.; but it was a soldier's job he did again that night, and for days and nights to follow. Once a shell burst in his path and smashed the radiator; he plugged it up with wood and kept her going. It is provoking to be obliged to add that I was not in the car at the time.

Nor did I thoroughly enjoy every minute of the hours I spent in it that Saturday night; there was far too much occasion both for pangs and fears. Though we had kept open longer than any other hut, and everybody else (who was going) had left the town before us, yet the rest had gone on foot and it seemed a villainy to pass them plodding in the stream of refugees outside the town. It is true they all boarded lorries at the earliest opportunity, and actually reached our common haven before us; but that did not make our performance less inglorious at the time. Nor had we any extenuating adventures on the way. The road, we understood, was being heavily shelled; unless the enemy slumbered and slept, it was bound to be; but I for one saw nothing of it. The Ford hood reduced the landscape to a few yards of moonlit track, and the Ford engine drowned all other noises of the night. But there was the perpetual apprehension of that which never once occurred. Wherever we stopped, it had been occurring freely. One of our huts, some kilometres out, was ringed with huge shell-holes; but none were added during the interminable time we waited in the road, while business was being transacted with which three of the four of us had nothing to do. I do not know which was greater, the relief of getting under way again, or the shame of leaving the crew of that hut to their fate.

Yet we had but to forget our own miserable skins and sensibilities, to remember we were only on-lookers, and be thankful to be there that night in any capacity whatsoever. For the straight French road whereon we travelled—the wrong way, for our sins!—was choked with strings of lorries and motor-'buses full of reinforcements for the battle-line; silent men, miles and miles of them, mostly invisible, load after load; all embussed, not a single company to be seen upon the march. It was weird, but it was gorgeous: the tranquil moon above, the tossing dust below, and these tall landships, packed with fighting-men, looming through by the hundred. This one, we kept saying, must be the last; but scarcely were we abreast, grazing her side, craning to make out the men behind her darkened ports, than another ship-load broke dimly through the dust, to tower above us in its turn.

Thousands and thousands of gallant hearts! Sometimes the men themselves fretted the top of a familiar 'bus—of course in khaki like its load—but for the most part they were out of sight inside. And—it may have been the drowning thud of their great engines, the noisier racket of our own—but not a human sound can I remember first or last. So they passed, speeding to the rescue; so they passed, how many to their reward! Louder than our throbbing engines, and louder than the guns they deadened, the fighting blood of England sang that night through all these arteries of France; and our own few drops danced with our tears, hurt as it might to rush by upon the other side.

What with one stoppage and another, and always going against the stream of heavy traffic, the thirty or forty kilometres must have taken us three or four hours; and there, as I was saying, were our poor pedestrians in port before us. It dispelled anxiety, if it did no more. But there was no end to our mean advantages; for the good easy men were making their beds upon the bare boards of the local Y.M.C.A., where we found them with the refugees from yet another group of forsaken huts, some eighty souls in all. They assured us there were no beds to be had in the place, that the Town Major had commandeered every mattress. But a cunning and influential veteran whispered another story in my private ear; and on the understanding that his surreptitious arrangements should include the mate of the Rest Hut, we adjourned with our friend in need to the best hotel in the town, whence after supper we were conducted to a still better billet. Here were not only separate beds, with sheets on them, but separate rooms with muslin curtains, marbled wash-stands, clocks and mirrors. It was true we had been forced to leave our heavy baggage at headquarters in our own poor town; and there had not been room in my despatch-case for any raiment for the night. But that was because I had refused to escape without my library records, whatever else was left behind. And the extensive contact with cool linen could not lessen the glow of virtue, on that solitary head, with which I stretched myself out in comfort inconceivable fifteen hours before.

The day, beginning with the shock received from the Scottish Padre at the head of the dungeon stairs, had been packed with surprise, disappointment, irritation, mortal apprehension and emotion more varied than any day of mine had ever yet brought forth. But I was physically tired out, and a great deal more stolid about it all that night than I feel now, six months after the event. The silence, I remember, was the only thing that troubled me, after those three days and nights of almost incessant shell-fire. But it was a joyous trouble—while it lasted. Hardly had I closed my eyes upon the moonlit muslin curtains, when I woke with a start to that unaltered scene. The only difference was the slightly irregular hum of an enemy aeroplane, and the noise of bombs bursting all too near our perfect billet.

IN THE DAY OF BATTLE

It was not my first acquaintance with the town, nor yet with the hotel to which our billet was affiliated. I had been there on a book-raid in better days. It was in that hotel I found the hero of the apopthegm: 'Once a soldier—always a civilian!' And now its dismal saloons were overflowing with essential civilians who might have been soldiers all their lives; only here and there could one detect a difference; all seemed equally imbued with the traditional nonchalance of the British officer in a tight place. But for their uniform, and their martial carriage, they might have been a festive gathering of the Old Boys of any Public School.

After breakfast we others sallied forth. The sun was still prematurely hot. The uninjured street was full not only of khaki, but of the townsfolk of both sexes, a new element to us in any but rare glimpses. Their Sunday faces betrayed no sign of special anxiety. The bells were tinkling peacefully for mass as we crossed the little river flowing close behind the backs of the houses, and climbed the grassy height on which the citadel stands bastioned. A party of British soldiers was camped in its chill shadow; many were washing at the stream below, their bodies white as milk between their trousers and their sunburnt necks. Some, I think, were actually bathing. They did not look like the battered remnant of a grand Battalion. Yet that was what they were.

We foregathered with one chip from the modern battle-axe: a Sergeant and old soldier who had been through all the war and through South Africa. The last three days beat all. There had never been anything to touch them. Masses had melted before his eyes. There they were, as thick as corn, one minute, and the next they lay in swathes, and the next again the swathes were one continuous stack of dead. The illustration was the Sergeant's, and I know the fine rolling countryside he got it from; but it was not the burden of his yarn. This came in so often, with an effect so variable, that I was puzzled, knowing the perverse levity of the type.

'No nation can stand it,' were the exact words more than once. 'No nation that ever was, can go on standing it.'

'Do you mean—?'

But I saw he didn't! The whites of his eyes were like an inner ring of brick-red skin, but it was their blue that flamed with sardonic humour.

'I mean the Germans!' cried he. 'No nation on earth can go on standing what they had to stand yesterday and the day before. It's not in human nature to go on standing it. I don't say as we didn't get it too....'

Nor could he, while telling us what the remnant in the tents and on the river-bank represented; but all such information was imparted in the tone of a man making an admission for the sake of argument or fair play. If I remember, the Sergeant had two wound-stripes under his pile of service chevrons. But he had borne more lives than a squad of cats. 'Each time I find I'm all right, I just shake 'ands with myself and carry on.' We got him to shake hands with us, and so parted with a diamond in human form.

Along the road below came the rag-time of a mediocre band; we hurried down and stood in a gateway to review a company of Australians marching into the town. This string of jewels was still unscattered by the fight, of the same high water as our south-country Sergeant, only different in cut and polish, if not of set sarcastic purpose. They were marching in their own way; no stride or swing about it; but a more subtle jauntiness, a kind of mincing strut, perhaps not unconsciously sinister and unconventional, an aggressive part of themselves. But what men! What beetling chests, what muscle-swollen sleeves, what dark, pugnacious, shaven faces! Here and there a pendulous moustache mourned the beard of some bushman of the old school; but no such adventitious aids could have improved upon the naked truculence of most of those mouths and chins. In their supercilious confidence they reminded me of the early Australian cricketers, of beardless Blackham, Boyles and Bonnors taking the field to mow down the flower of English cricket, in the days when those were our serious wars. How I had hated the type as a schoolboy sitting open-mouthed and heart-broken at the Oval! How I had feared it as a hobble-de-hoy in the bush itself! But, in the day of battle, could there have been a better sight than this potential band of bush-rangers and demon bowlers? Not to my glasses; nor one more bitter for the mate of the Rest Hut, thrice rejected from those very ranks.

We wandered idly in their wake; and the next sight that I remember, though it may not have been that morning, was almost as cheering in its very different way. It was the spectacle of a single German prisoner, being marched through the streets by a single British soldier with fixed bayonet. The prisoner was an N.C.O., and a fine defiant brute, marching magnificently just to show us. But his was not the hate that conceals hate; he was the incarnation of the ineffable hymn, with his quick-firing eyes and the high angle of his powerful chin. Physically our man could not compare with him. And that seemed symbolical, at a moment when signs and symbols were in some request.

Then there were the men one had met before. Congested as it was with traffic to and from the fighting, this little town was even more a rendezvous for old acquaintance than the one from which we had beaten our compulsory retreat. I was always running into somebody I had known of old or through his people. One glorious young man, who had been much upon my mind, came into the restaurant where we were having lunch on the Tuesday. His eyes were clear but strained, his ears loaded with yellow dust that toned artistically with his skin and hair. He said he had had his first sleep for five nights—under a railway arch. Before the war he had been up at Cambridge, and a very eminent Blue; if I said what he had it for, and what ribbon he was wearing now, I might as well break my rule and name him outright. But there had been three big brothers, then; now there was only this one left—and at one time not much of him. It did my heart good to see him here—looking as if he had never known a day's illness, or the pain of wounds or grief—looking a young god if there was one in France that day.

But it was not only for his own or for his family's sake that the mere sight of this splendid fellow was such a joy. The things he stood for were more precious than any life or group of lives. He stood for the generation which has been wiped out almost to a boy, as I knew it; he stood for his brothers, and for all our sons who made their sacrifice at once; he stood for the English games, and for those who had seemed to live for games, but who jumped into the King's uniform quicker than they ever changed into flannels in their lives. 'It is the one good thing the war has done—to give public-school fellows a chance—they are the one class who are enjoying themselves in this war.' So wrote one whose early innings was of the shortest; and though it was a boyish boast, and they were not the only class by any means, I should like to know which other was quite as valuable when the war, too, was in its infancy? In each and every country, by one means or the other, the men were to be had: only our Public Schools could have furnished off-hand an army of natural officers, trained to lead, old in responsibility, and afraid of nothing in the world but fear itself. There were very few of the first lot left last March, and now there are many fewer. Of one particular Eton and Harrow match, I believe it can be said that not half-a-dozen of the twenty-two players are now alive. It was something to meet so noble a survivor, still leading in battle as he had learnt to lead at school and college, both on and off the field.

Nor had one to hang about hotels and restaurants, or camps or the street corners, to see men straight from the fight or just going in, and to take fresh heart from theirs. The chief local Y.M.C.A. was full of both kinds, one more appealing than the other. It was perhaps the least conscious appeal ever made to human heart; for men are proud in the day of battle, and they are also mighty busy with their own affairs. What pocket stores they were laying in! What sanguine reserves of tobacco and cigarettes! That was a heartening sign. But there were no foreboding faces that I could see. It is one of the strong points of the inner soldier that he never thinks it is his turn; but if shell or bullet 'has his name on it,' it will 'see him off,' as he also puts it. Some call this fatalism. I call it Faith. It is their plain way of bowing to the Will of God. But the only bow I saw was over the long last letters many were writing, as though the bugle was already blowing for them, as though they well knew what it meant. There was no looking unmoved upon those bent backs and hurrying hands.

Nor were they the most poignant figures; it was the men who had been in it that one could not keep one's eyes off. Those we had seen bathing in the morning were nothing to them. They had a night's rest behind them; these were brands still smoking from the fire. Dirty as dustmen, red-eyed, and with the growth of all these days upon their haggard faces, some sat at the tables, eating and drinking like men who had just discovered their own emptiness; and many lay huddled on the floor, as on the battle-field itself, filling the hut with its very atmosphere. To step over them, and to sit with the men who had a mind to talk, was to get into the red heart of the thing that was going on.

Not that they had very much to tell; all were hazy as to what had happened; but all agreed it was the worst thing they had been through yet, and all bore out our Sunday morning friend, that it was worse for the enemy than for anybody else. This unanimity was remarkable; especially if you consider, first the military history of that last ten days in March, and secondly the fact that none of these unwounded stalwarts was there for a normal reason. Each stood for scores or hundreds who had gone under in the fight, or been taken prisoner. Yet it was worse for the enemy! Yet we were going to win! I cannot swear to the statement in those words, but it was implicit in their every utterance, and emphatic in the things they never said. For though I brought biscuits to many, and sat while they steeped them in their mugs and gulped them down, not a first syllable of complaint reached my ears. On that I would take my stand in any witness-box. And a Y.M.C.A. man knows; they trust us, and speak their minds.

Often in the winter 'peace-time,' as hinted early in these notes, I have seen men shudder at the prospect of the trenches, heard bitter murmurs at the mud and misery, and have done my best to answer the natural cry: 'When is this dreadful war going to finish? It will never be finished by fighting!' There was nothing of that sort to cope with now. In the winter I have heard lamentations for the stray man killed by a sniper or a stray shell. There was the case of the Lewis gunner who had earned his special leave; there was 'the best wee sergeant,' and there were others. But there was none of that now that men were falling by the thousand; not from a single one of these ravenous, red-eyed survivors. You may say it was their hunger, weariness, and consequent insensibility, the acquiescence of the sleeper in the snow. But they were full of confidence phlegmatic yet serene. They were on the winning side; there was never a doubt of it on their lips or in their eyes; and with us they had no reason to keep their doubts to themselves. They had voiced them freely in the winter. But now they had no doubts to voice.

I do not propound their perspicacity or postulate an instinct they did not claim themselves. I merely state a fact from observation of these handfuls of men in the first days of the great crisis. That was the way they reacted against the greatest enemy success since the first month of the war. It is the English way, and always has been. And they happen to be busy finishing the old sequel as I write.

Yet if you had seen their eyes! I remember as a little boy seeing Lady Butler's 'Charge of the Light Brigade' at my first Academy. I am not sure that I have looked upon the canvas since, but the wild-eyed central figure, 'back from the mouth of Hell,' rises up before me after forty years. There is, to be sure, only the most odious of comparisons between his heroic stand and the posture of my friends, who were not posing for a Victorian battle-piece, but bolting biscuits and spilling tea on a Y.M.C.A. table in modern France. Nevertheless, some of them had those eyes.

OTHER OLD FELLOWS

It was pleasant one morning to hear a sudden voice at my elbow: 'How's the Rest Hut?' and to find at least one of its regular frequenters still whole and hearty, in the press outside this teeming Y.M.C.A. But a more embarrassing encounter occurred the same day and on the same too public spot.

It began in the hut, with a couple of sad young Jocks, who were like to be sad, as they might have said; but they only smiled in wry yet not unhumorous resignation. Their story was that of thousands upon the imperative stoppage of all leave. These two had started off on theirs, and were going aboard at Boulogne when headed back to their Battalion, which they had now to find. It chanced to be one of those to which I had helped to minister in the sunken road at Christmas. They remembered the Cocoa Man, as I had been called there, but in the morning they were not demonstrative.

About mid-day we met again, and as I say, in the surging crowd outside the Y.M.C.A. This time the case was sadly altered; the hapless pair had been consoling themselves at another spring, and were at the warm-hearted stage. Nothing was now too good for the poor Cocoa Man, no compliment too wildly hyperbolical. Falling with their unabated forces upon both his hands, only stopping short of the actual neck, they greeted him as 'a brave mon' in that concourse of braves, and proceeded to embroider the charge with unconscionable detail.

'Thairty-five yarrds from the Gairmans,' declared one, 'this ol' feller was teemin' cocoa in the trenches. I'm tellin' ye! Lash C'rishmash—mind ye—shnow an' ische! Thairty-five yarrds from the Gairmans—strike me dead!'

A vindictive Deity might well have taken him at his word, for dividing the real distance by more than ten. But nothing came of it except a murmur of general incredulity, obsequiously confirmed by the Cocoa Man, and from the other Jock's wagging head a sentimental echo: 'Thish ol' feller! Thish ol' feller!' he could only say for the pavement's benefit.

'Why was I there?' demanded the spokesman, with a rhetorical thump upon his chest. 'Dis-cip-line—dis-cip-line—only reason I was there. But this ol' feller—'

'Thish ol' feller!' screamed the other, in a paroxysm of affection; and when I had eventually retrieved both hands I left them singing my longevity in those terms, like a catch, and took my blushes to a safer part of the town.

'I've given them a bitty,' whispered one of our ministers, who had assisted my escape, 'and told them to go away and get something to eat.'

And the sly carnal wisdom of the advice, no less than the charity which made it practicable, left a good taste in the mouth. It was the kind of thing I ventured to think we wanted in our workers. In any community of sinners there is room for the saint who will help a man to get sober sooner than scold him for getting drunk.

Not that I saw above half-a-dozen tipsy men in all the huts that I was ever in. They were to be seen, no doubt, but they did not come our way. The soldier who seeks the Y.M. in his cups is not a hardened case. He is the last person to be discouraged, as he will be the first to deplore his imprudence in the morning. I have heard a splendid young New Zealander speak of the lapse that had cost him his stripes as though nobody had ever made so dire a fool of himself. That is the kind of notion to scout even at the cost of a high line in these matters. It is possible to make too much of the virtues that come easily to ourselves; and to the average Y.M.C.A. man the cardinal virtues seemed very like second nature. This is not covert irony, but a simple fact which, for that matter, ought hardly to have been otherwise, since most of us were ministers of one denomination or another. The minority were apt to feel, but were not necessarily justified in feeling, that a more liberal admixture of 'sinful laymen' might have put us, as a body, even more intimately in touch with the men than we undoubtedly were.

Chief, however, among the virtues of my comrades, I think any unprejudiced observer would have placed that of Courage. There were now no fewer than eighty of us, all leaves before the wind of war, blown helter-skelter into this little town that must be nameless. We had come off all sorts and sizes of trees, down to the most sensitive and frailest; but from the first squall to the last we were permitted to face, and throughout these days of precarious shelter, in many ways a higher test, I never saw a man among us outwardly the worse for nerves. And be it known that the small personal escapes and excitements recorded in these notes, were as nothing to the full-size adventures of a great many of our refugees. In outlying huts, cheek by jowl with the camps they served, the shelling had been far heavier and more direct than the officers of the Rest Hut had been privileged to undergo; the responsibility had been much greater, and the means of escape not to be compared with ours. Little home-made dug-outs, under the hut itself, had been their nearest approach to our vaulted dungeon, a tattoo of shrapnel their variety of shell-music. Whole walls had been blown in on them, men killed and wounded under the riddled roof. Some had suffered even more from a bodyguard of our own guns than from the enemy; one reverend gentleman declared in writing that his 'hut reeled like a ship in a great sea.'

Another wrote: 'A wave of gas entered our domain and we had a season of intense coughing and sneezing, also watering of eyes. Thinking it was but a passing wave of gas from our own guns, we did not use our respirators, but reaching up to a box of sweets I distributed them to my comrades, and we lay sucking sweets to take away the taste.' (This was a Baptist minister with a South African ribbon, and not the man to lie long doing anything.) 'After breakfast I called upon the Artillery Officers to offer my staff to make hot cocoa and supply biscuits during the morning for the hard-worked gun-teams, an offer which he gratefully accepted. I then made my way up to the dressing-station to see if the Medical Officer required our services for the walking wounded. His reply being in the affirmative, I took stock of the equipment we had on the spot, then went back to bring up all necessary articles, also my comrades. The small hut we have near the dressing-station for this work was being so hotly shelled that the M.O. would not allow us to remain there, so we worked outside the dressing-station door, a little more sheltered, but still exposed to shell-fire. We comforted the wounded, gave them hot tea and free cigarettes. A lull occurred during the morning in our work, so Mr. — returned to make the cocoa for the gun-teams, Mr. — remained to carry on at the dressing-station, and I returned to clear the cash-boxes, fill my pockets with rescued paper-money, prepared again for emergency.... We continued our work with the wounded, and as the same increased in number, I then assisted in bandaging the smaller wounds, having knowledge of that kind of work. Later, the A.P.M. gave me his field-glasses and asked me to act as observer and report to him every change in the progress of the battle of the ridges. This was most interesting work, but meant constant exposure. One of our aeroplanes sounded its hooter and dropped a message about 600 yards away. On reporting it I was asked to cross over and see that the message was delivered to the correct battery.'

This was a man! But do not forget he was also a Baptist minister on a four-months furlough at the front. 'Once a soldier!' he too may have said after his first campaign, and clinched it by entering his ministry; but here he was in his pious prime, excelling his lay youth in deeds of gallantry, and covering our civilian heads with his reflected glory. No wonder he 'heard from two sources that my work on that day received mention in military dispatches.' Let us hope it did. 'If true,' he makes haste to add, 'the work of my two colleagues is as much deserving.' But who inspired them? Before they turned their backs, 'the advancing Germans were only about 700 yards away. Securing some of our goods, we decided to retire upon — for the night and return if possible the next day.' The last six words italicise themselves.

The party went out of the frying-pan into heavier fire further back: 'Soon after we had retired to rest the Germans commenced to bombard the place with high velocity shells from long range.... A Lieutenant in our hut went to the door, but reeled back immediately with a shattered arm. A Corporal outside received a nasty wound in the shoulder. We set to work bandaging the wounds of these men and making them comfortable while others went to obtain a conveyance. There was no shelter, so after the wounded were safely on their way to a C.C.S. we lay down in our blankets, considering it as easy to be shelled in the warm as standing in the cold'—more wine that needs no printer's bush. Later, he relieved the leader of a very hot hut indeed, where he had for colleague 'one who was calm in the hour of danger.' Here the congenial pair 'were able to carry on for four days, when the order came for us to evacuate. We distributed our stock of goods to the soldiers, then closed up. That night we lay in our blankets counting the bursting shells around us at three shells per minute.' On their arrival in our common port, naturally not before, 'the effects of the gas at — began to make themselves felt, and I was ordered by the Medical Officer to take a week's complete rest.' One wonders if a rest was better earned in all those terrific days.

The document from which I have been quoting is only one of many placed at my disposal. It is typical of them all, exceptional solely in the telling simplicity of the narrator. The writer was not our only minister who came through the fire pure gold; he was not even the only Baptist minister. One there was, the gentlest of souls, whose heroic story I may yet make shift to tell, though it deserves the hand of Mr. Service or of 'Woodbine Willie.' Such were the men I had the honour of working with last winter, and of such their adventures as against the personal experiences it was necessary to recount first or else not at all. I confess they make my Rest Hut look a little too restful as I set them down; for there we were wonderfully spared the tangible horrors of the situation; but many of these others, as little used to bloodshed as ourselves, had left a shambles behind them, and looked upon the things that haunt a mind.

And yet, as I began by saying, not a man of them showed shaken nerves, or what mattered more to those of us who had seen less, a shaken faith. Therein they were not only worthy of the men they had served so devotedly to the end, but of the sublime tradition it was theirs to uphold. It was a great matter that there should not have been one heart among us so faint as to affect another, that we should have carried ourselves at least outwardly as I think we did. But to some of us it seemed a yet greater matter, in the days of anti-climax and reaction now in store, that those to whom we were entitled to look for spiritual support did not fail us in a single instance.

THE REST CAMP—AND AFTER

Y.M.C.A. work was over for the time being in the fighting areas. Hundreds of huts and mountains of stores had been abandoned or destroyed. What was to be done with the six or seven dozen of us, now thoroughly superfluous men (and as many more in other centres), was the immediate problem. It was solved by the High Command putting at our disposal an Army rest-camp on the coast.

Thither we all started by rail on the evening of Tuesday, March 26th. Ten minutes after our train left, the station was heavily bombed; half-an-hour later we were lying low in a cutting, under a mercilessly full moon, but perhaps in deeper shadow than we supposed, while a German aeroplane scoured the sky for mischief. There was an Anti-Aircraft Battery also concealed about the district; thanks to its activities, we were at length able to proceed with less fear of molestation. But only fitfully; the full moon saw to that. It was as light as noonday through smoked glasses, and very soon our train was hiding in the next wood that happened to intersect the line.

Did we waste time talking about it, discussing our chances, or mildly anathematising our last-straw luck? Not for many minutes; at least, not in the bare truck round which some fifty of us squatted on our baggage. We had begun the last stage of our exodus in a certain fashion; and in that fashion we went on—and on. Before we were five minutes out, one of them had struck up a hymn, and we had sung it with all our lungs and hearts. Another and another followed; and in the stoppages, after a human peep at the sky, and a silence broken by the beat of the destroyer's engine, there was always some exalted voice to lead us yet again, and a stentorian following every time. Though the tunes were often strange to me, and to my mind no improvement on the ones I wanted, the hymns themselves were the old hymns that take a man back to his old home and his old school. Each was like a bottle charged with the essence of some ancient scene. One savoured the scents of vanished rooms, heard the sound of voices long past singing or long ago stilled; forgotten influences, childish promptings, looks and thoughts and sayings, came leaping out of the dead past into that dark truck hiding for dear life in a wood. And of all the unreal situations I was ever in—or invented, for that matter—this at last struck me as about the most unconvincing and far-fetched. Yet at the same time, like all else that really matters, it seemed the most natural thing in the world: as though the whole history of mankind had not led up to the horrors and splendours of this stupendous war more inevitably than our fifty life-lines converged in that truck-load of brave, faithful, hymn-singing men.

Then a hymn would end, and there would be sometimes as much as a minute of natural talk and normal thinking. But it was like the lorries full of fighting-men in the moonlit dust; always a new leader filled the breach; and the officers of the Rest Hut had long been stolid listeners when we stopped once more, not to hide, but at some station, and that weary pair sneaked out into another truck. Here there were but other two before them: a sardonic Anglican, and a young man enviably asleep under less covering than would have soothed our thinner blood. Side by side we cowered upon a packing-case, a Rest Hut blanket about our legs, and discussed the secular situation over a pipe. Almost the last thing we two had heard in the town was a whisper about the German cavalry; a rumour so sensational that we were keeping it to ourselves; but it only confirmed the mate in his prophetic conviction that the fools were just cutting their own throats deeper with every mile they advanced. That was his hymn; not a stage of our flight had he failed to beguile with the grim refrain; but in the truck I seem to recall a wilder dream of getting into some dead man's uniform, if the other folly went much further, and risking a firing-party for one blow at a Boche by fair or foul. It was perhaps as well that we were going beyond the reach of any such desperate temptations.

The Rest Camp was on a chilly plateau at the mouth of the Somme: it might have been the Murrambidgee for all the warfare within reach. A few faint flashes claimed our wistful attention on a clear night, but I have heard the guns better here in Sussex. On the other hand, it was a military camp, laid out on scientific principles that appealed to the camp-following spirit, and military discipline kept us on our acquired mettle. I had not slept under canvas for thirty years, and rather dreaded it, especially as the weather had turned cold and unsettled. A tent in the rain had perhaps more terrors for many of us than a snug hut under occasional shell-fire; but few if any were the worse for the experience. Indeed, the chief drawback was an appetite out of all proportion to available rations; but, though tempers were at times on edge, and fists clenched in the bacon queue, on one of our few bacon mornings, no grumbling disgraced the board. We reminded ourselves and each other of the lads we had left to bear the brunt, and we started our humdrum days with vociferous jocosity in the wash-house.

Easter was upon us before we were fairly settled, or a tent pitched large enough to hold us all; and it was 'in sundry places,' indeed, that we mobilised as a congregation. One was the open shed in which we shivered over meals, and one the camp shower-baths. But on Easter Day, which was fine and bright, all adjourned to a neighbouring wood, then breaking into bud and song; and sitting or leaning in a circle against the trees, at the intersection of two green rides, we held our service in Nature's sanctuary. In that ring of unmilitary men in khaki there were few who had not been nearer violent death than ever in their lives before, very few but were prepared to face it afresh at the first chance, one at least who was soon to be killed behind his counter; and presently a young man standing in our midst, an Anglican with a Nonconformist gift of speech, brought the spring morning home to our hearts, filled them with thankfulness for our lot and trust in the issue, and pride of sacrifice, and love of Him Who showed the way, in a sermon one would not have missed for the best they were getting in London at that hour. It was not the only fine sermon we had in the Rest Camp; and wonderful it was to hear the same simple note struck so often, albeit from different angles of the Christian faith, and so seldom forced. We must have had representatives of all the English-spoken Churches, save and except the parent of them all; constantly an Anglican and a Dissenter would officiate together, with many a piquant compromise between their respective usages; but when it came to preaching, they were like searchlights trained from divers quarters upon the same central fact of Christianity. The separate beams might taper off into the night, but high overhead they met and mingled in a single splendour.

But there was one minister who took no part; he lay too sick in our tent; and yet his mere record is the sermon I remember best. He was that other Baptist already mentioned, a shy bachelor of fifty, the most diffident and (one might have thought) least resolute of men. A lad he loved had come out and been killed; the impulse took him to follow and throw himself into the war in the only capacity open to his years. The Y.M.C.A. is the refuge of those consciously or unconsciously in quest of this anodyne. We had met at my first hut, where he had slaved many days as an extra hand. Never was one of us so deferential towards the men; never were they served with a more intense solicitude, or addressed across the counter with so many marks of respect. 'Sir,' he never failed to call them to their faces, or 'this gentleman' when invoking expert intervention. That gentleman, being one, never smiled; but we did, sometimes, in our room. Then one Sunday I persuaded him to preach. It was a revelation. The hut had heard nothing simpler, manlier, straighter from the shoulder; and the war, not just then the safest subject, was finely and bravely treated, both in the sermon and the final prayer. A fighting sermon and a fighting prayer, for all the gentle piety that formed the greater part, and all the sensitive mannerism which would never make us smile again.

At that time our outpost in the support line, scene of my Christmas outing, had been running a good many weeks; and its popularity as a holiday resort was not imperceptibly upon the wane. Most of us had tasted its fearful joys, and there were no offers for a second helping; it was emphatically a thing to have done rather than the thing to do again. It came to the Baptist's turn, and when his week was up there was a genuine difficulty in relieving him, one or two on the rota having fallen sick. Our young commandant went up to ask if he would mind doing an extra day or two. Mind! It was his one desire; he was as happy as a king—and he had quite transformed the place. The tiny hut was no longer the pig-sty described in an earlier note; it was as neat and spotless as an old maid's sanctum. The urns were like burnished silver. The fire never smoked. The bed had been brought in from the unspeakable tunnel under the sand-bags; it was as dry as a bone, and curtained off at its own end of the cabin. All these improvements the Baptist had wrought single-handed, besides fending and cooking for himself: no Battalion Headquarters for him! An extra week was just what he had been longing for; in point of fact, he stayed four weeks on end, as against my four paltry days!

Shells arrived in due course; death happened at the door; men grievously wounded staggered in for first aid; the lengthening days kept him fireless till evening; but the cocoa had never been so well made, or so continuous the supply. Once a big shell burst within a yard of the grassy roof, on the very edge of the high ground of which the roof was a colourable extension. It brought down all the mugs and urns and condensed-milk tins with a run; and that day we did see the Baptist at our mid-day board. 'It shook me up a bitty,' he confessed with his shy laugh; but back he went in the afternoon; and illness alone restored him to us when the month was up.

But the gem of his performance was an act of moral gallantry: and here is needed the Rough Rhyme of a Padre or of a Red Cross Man. One cold night a Sergeant-Major—Regimental, I do believe—honoured the cabin with his presence, only to fire a burst of improper language at the weather and the war. The

Baptist, whom we may figure on the verge of genuflexion before the august guest, lost not a moment in standing up to him.

'You can't talk like that here, sir!' he cried with stern simplicity. 'It's not allowed!'

'Can't,' if you please, and 'not allowed'! You picture the audience settling down to the dreadful drama, hear the cold shudders of the callow, see the turkey-cock turning an appropriate purple. He very soon showed what he could do; but it was no longer a spontaneous or such a glib display. The rum that happened somehow to be in him seems to have had something to do with this; but not, it may be, as much as the Sergeant-Major pretended; and the torpor that rather suddenly supervened I diagnose as the ready resource of an expert in camouflage. Better gloriously drunk than ignominiously admonished by an unprintable hiatus of a Y.M. Padre!

So a party of muscular volunteers escorted the S.M. to his dug-out. But the next day he returned alone, crisp-footed and square-jawed, apparently to put the Baptist in his place for ever. Exactly what followed, that gentle hero was not the man to relate. Again one pictures Peeping Tommies exposing themselves on the sunken road to see the fun, perhaps the murder; but what I really believe they might have seen, before many minutes were up, was the spectacle of the two protagonists upon their knees.

Stranger things have been happening, even on that sunken road of ours. It was lost to us in those very days of the Army Rest Camp; it had not been recovered when I was busy expatiating on its Christmas charms; its recovery was one of the first loose stones in the avalanche of vast events which has caught me up.... And now they say the war is over! To have seen something of it all in the last dark hour—and nothing since—is to find even more than the old war-time difficulty in believing half one hears. One has too many fixed ideas and violent impressions, not only of those four months, but of these four years: a man has to clear his own entanglements before he can begin to advance with such times. In the meantime the patter about Indemnities and Demobilisation leaves him cold. Demobilisation will have to begin nearer home than charity, in the armies of our thoughts; and some are not as highly disciplined as others, some hearts too sore to enter as they would into this Peace.

For them there is still the Y.M.C.A. That little force of camp-followers still holds the field, has nothing to say to any Armistice, may well have started its most strenuous campaign. With the Armies of Occupation its work will hardly be the romantic enterprise it was; with all the danger, most of the glamour will have departed; but the deeper attractions are the less adventitious, while the Rhine at any rate should provide some piquant novelties in place of old excitements. The grand fleet of huts will soon be anchored there—including, as I hope, the new Rest Hut that was to have been tucked up close behind the Line. Once more before each counter there will be the old press of matchless manhood and humanity; neater and sprucer, I make no doubt, but otherwise neither more nor less like conquering heroes than their old unconquerable selves; and just once more, behind the counter, the chance of a lifetime, but the last chance, for 'sinful laymen' of the milder sort!

Will it be taken? Are our courageous ministers to have the last field practically to themselves, or will a few mere men of the world even now step in, if only for the honour of the laity? They would if they knew what the work is like and what it may be made, how free a hand is given one, how generously one is met by all concerned, and the modicum of spiritual equipment essential if only that modicum be sincere. Pre-war notions about the Young Men's Christian Association still militate a little against the Y.M.C.A. for all the halo of success attaching to those capitals; but hear a soldier from the front upon the 'Y.M.' tout court, and his affectionate abbreviation of an abbreviation will in itself tell you something of the institution as it is to-day. It has meant rather more to him than 'tea and prayer in equal parts'; yet that conception still prevails in superior circles. Quite lately I heard a dignitary of the Established Church speak with pain of a brilliant young Oxford man of his acquaintance, who, rejected of the Army, must needs be 'giving out tea in some tent in France!' It seemed to him a truly shocking waste of fine material; but if that young man was not giving out a great deal more than creature comforts, and getting at least as good as he gave, then it was a still more wanton waste of an opportunity which the finest young man alive might have been proud to seize.

The truth is, of course, that no man is too good for this job. He may be a specialist, and more valuable to the community where he is than he would be (to the community) in a Y.M.C.A. or a Church Army hut. He may be a Cabinet Minister, a Bishop, or a Judge: that does not make him too good to minister to the men who have borne the brunt of this war: it only makes him too busy and perhaps too old. One must not even now be extra liable to 'die of winter,' as the Tynesider said, nor yet too dainty about bed and board. But the better the man, the better he will do this work, the more he will bring to it, the more he will find in it; the greater will be his tact, the greater his loving-kindness and humility; the readier will he be to recognise many a better man than himself in our noble rank-and-file—to learn all they have to teach him in patience and naturalness, unselfishness and simplicity—and to perceive the higher service involved in serving them, even across a counter.

To Him Who made the Heavens move and cease not in their motion—
To Him Who leads the haltered tides twice a day round ocean—
Let His name be magnified in all poor folks' devotion!

Not for Prophecies or Powers, Visions, Gifts or Graces,
But the unrelenting hours that grind us in our places,
With the burden on our backs, the smile upon our faces.

Not for any miracle of easy loaves and fishes,
But for work against our will and waiting 'gainst our wishes—
Such as gathering up the crumbs and cleaning dirty dishes.

It may or may not be that Mr. Kipling is thinking of the Y.M.C.A. I do not know the title of his poem, or whether it has yet appeared elsewhere, or another line of it. These lines I owe to his kindness, and as usual they crystallise all that one was trying to say. But to some of us the crumbs that fell were a feast of fine humanity, and great indeed was his reward who gathered them.

E. W. Hornung – A Short Biography

Ernest William Hornung was born on 7th June 1866 at Cleveland Villas, Marton, Middlesbrough. He was the third son, and youngest of eight children, to John Peter Hornung and his wife Harriet née Armstrong.

By the age of 13 Hornung had joined St Ninian's Preparatory School in Moffat, Dumfriesshire before enrolling at the exclusive Uppingham School, in Rutland, in 1880.

Hornung suffered from a general state of bad health, including asthma and poor eyesight but managed to be well-liked at school and to develop a life-long passion of cricket. He loved to play despite the obvious fact that his talents were rather limited.

At 17 his health worsened, and he left Uppingham to travel to Australia, where a sunnier climate was deemed to be better for his various ailments.

Upon arriving he worked as a tutor to the Parsons family in Mossgiel, in New South Wales. As well as teaching he spent time working in remote sheep stations in the outback and began to contribute materials to the weekly magazine; The Bulletin. It was also at this time that he began work on his first novel.

After two years of very valuable life experiences Hornung returned to England in February 1886, a few months before the death of his father, in November, whose deteriorating business interests had become a constant worry.

Hornung found work in London as a journalist and story writer. In 1887 he published his first story under his own name, 'Stroke of Five', which appeared in Belgravia magazine. His work as a journalist coincided with the reign of terror brought about by Jack the Ripper's grisly murders. From this Hornung developed an interest in criminal behaviour.

He had completed the manuscript of the novel he brought back from Australia and, between July and November 1890, the story, 'A Bride from the Bush', was published in five parts in the respected Cornhill Magazine. It was released later that year in book form. This, his first novel, was well received by critics.

Hoping to further his talents in cricket Hornung, in 1891, became a member of two cricket clubs: the Idlers, whose members included Arthur Conan Doyle and Jerome K. Jerome, and the Strand club.

Hornung knew Doyle's sister, Constance ('Connie') from when he had visited Portugal. Connie was described as attractive, "with pre-Raphaelite looks ... the most sought-after of the Doyle daughters".

They were married on 27th September 1893, although Doyle was not at the wedding and relations between the two writers were occasionally difficult. The Hornung's had their only child, a son, Arthur Oscar (but always called just Oscar), in 1895.

In 1894 Doyle and Hornung began work on a play for Henry Irving, on the subject of boxing; Doyle was, at first, eager to begin and paid Hornung a £50 advance but then withdrew before the first act had been completed: the play was never finished.

Like Hornung's first novel, 'Tiny Luttrell' had Australia as a backdrop and the device of an Australian woman in a culturally alien environment. This theme ran through his next four novels: 'The Boss of Taroomba' (1894), 'The Unbidden Guest' (1894), 'Irralie's Bushranger' (1896), in this Hornung introduced the character of Stingaree, an Oxford-educated, Australian gentleman thief. In 'The Rogue's March' (1896) Hornung began to show a growing fascination with the motivation behind criminal behaviour and was sympathetic to the criminal hero as a victim of events. It was different thinking but caused some consternation for others.

In 1898 Hornung's mother died and he dedicated his next book, a series of short stories; Some Persons Unknown, to her memory.

Later that year Hornung and Connie spent six months in Posillipo, Italy. An account of this trip was published in the May 1899 issue of the Cornhill Magazine.

The fictional character Stingaree was re-written to become his most famous creation; A. J. Raffles; the gentleman thief, first used in six short stories published in 1898 in Cassell's Magazine. Modelled on George Cecil Ives, a Cambridge-educated criminologist and talented cricketer who, like Raffles, lived in the Albany, a gentlemen's only residence in Mayfair. The first tale of the series 'In the Chains of Crime' was published in June that year, titled 'The Ides of March'.

Another account adds to the richness by asserting that Raffles and his sidekick, Bunny Manders, were based not only on Doyle's Holmes and Watson but also on his friends Oscar Wilde and his lover, Lord Alfred Douglas. Whatever the exact amalgam the characters were warmly embraced by the reading public who turned it into both a popular and financial success, although some critics echoed Doyle's own fears of the dubious nature of a criminal being used as a hero.

In early 1899, the Hornung's returned to London, and resided in Pitt Street, West Kensington, for the next six years.

After publishing two novels, 'Dead Men Tell No Tales' (1899) and 'Peccavi' (1900), Hornung published a second collection of Raffles stories, 'The Black Mask', in 1901. The critics again complained about the criminal aspect. The public who bought them had no such qualms.

In 1903 Hornung collaborated with Eugène Presbrey to write a four-act play, 'Raffles, The Amateur Cracksman', which was based on two previously published short stories, 'Gentlemen and Players' and 'The Return Match'. The play was first performed at the Princess Theatre, New York, on 27th October 1903 and ran for 168 performances.

In 1905, after publishing four other books in the interim, Hornung brought back the character Stingaree. Later that year, in response to public demand he published a third collection of Raffles stories in 'A Thief in the Night', in which Manders relates some of the earlier adventures he had had with Raffles.

In 1909 the final Raffles story was published, the full-length novel 'Mr. Justice Raffles'. It was poorly received. The Observer reviewer asking if "Hornung is perhaps a little tired of Raffles".

It seems not. That same year he partnered with Charles Sansom for the play 'A Visit From Raffles', which was performed in November that year at the Brixton Empress Theatre, London.

Hornung turned away from Raffles thereafter, and in February 1911 published 'The Camera Fiend', a thriller whose narrator is an asthmatic cricket enthusiast and his attempts to photograph the soul as it leaves the body. This was followed by 'Fathers of Men' (1912) and 'The Thousandth Woman' (1913) before 'Witching Hill' (1913), a collection of eight short stories in which he introduced the characters Uvo Delavoye and the narrator Gillon. In 1914 his fictional works ceased with 'The Crime Doctor'.

His son, Oscar, left Eton College in 1914, and was due to proceed to King's College, Cambridge later that year. However, the terrors of WWI were about to unleash themselves all over Europe. Oscar volunteered, and was commissioned into the Essex Regiment. He was killed, aged a mere 20, at the Second Battle of Ypres on 6th July 1915.

Although heartbroken Hornung edited and issued privately a collection of Oscar's letters home under the title 'Trusty and Well Beloved', in 1916.

Around this time Hornung himself joined an anti-aircraft unit. He also joined the YMCA and did volunteer work in England for soldiers on leave. In March 1917 he visited France, writing a poem about his experience afterwards—something he had been doing more frequently since Oscar's death—and a collection of his war poetry, 'Ballad of Ensign Joy', was published later that year.

In July 1917 Hornung's poem, 'Wooden Crosses', was published in The Times, and in September, 'Bond and Free' appeared. A few months later he was accepted as a volunteer in a YMCA canteen and library just a few miles behind the Front Line.

Hornung was concerned about support for pacifism among troops and wrote to Connie about it. She spoke to Doyle and, rather than discussing it with Hornung, he informed the military authorities. Hornung was naturally angered by Doyle's action and relations between the two men were further strained as a result. He continued to work at the library until a German offensive overran the British positions and he was forced to retreat, firstly to Amiens and then, in April, back to England. He stayed in England until November 1918, when he again took up his YMCA duties, establishing a rest hut and library in Cologne.

In 1919 Hornung's account of his time spent in France, 'Notes of a Camp-Follower on the Western Front', was published. Doyle later wrote of the book that "there are parts of it which are brilliant in their vivid portrayal". That year Hornung also published his third and final volume of poetry, 'The Young Guard'.

Hornung finished his YMCA work and returned to England in early 1919. He worked on a new novel but was hampered by poor health. But Connie's was of greater concern. In February 1921 they took a holiday in the south of France to recuperate. Whilst travelling there on the train Hornung fell ill with a chill that progressed to influenza and finally pneumonia.

Ernest William Hornung died on 22nd March 1921, aged 54.

He was buried in Saint-Jean-de-Luz, in the south of France, in a grave adjacent to that of George Gissing.

E. W. Hornung – A Concise Bibliography

Periodicals
Stroke of Five (1887, Belgravia)
Spoilt Negative (1887, Belgravia)
Nettleship's Score (January 1890, Cornhill Magazine)
A Bride From the Bush (5 Parts. July-Nov, Cornhill Magazine, 1890)
Thunderbolt's Mate (4 Parts. March 1892, Chambers's Journal)
Kenyon's Innings (April 1892, Longman's Magazine)

The Burrawurra Brand (November 1893, The Idler)
The Unbidden Guest (6 Parts. May-Oct 1894, Longman's Magazine)
The Governess at Greenbush (4 parts. February 1895, Chambers's Journal)
After the Fact (3 Parts. January 1896, Chambers's Journal)
The Ides of March (June 1898, Cassell's Magazine)
A Villa in a Vineyard (May 1899, Cornhill Magazine)
No Sinicure: More Adventures of the Amateur Cracksman (January 1901, Scribner's Magazine)
A Jubilee Present: More Adventures of the Amateur Cracksman (February 1901, Scribner's Magazine)
The Fate of Faustina: More Adventures of the Amateur Cracksman (March 1901, Scribner's Magazine)
The Last Laugh: More Adventures of the Amateur Cracksman (April 1901, Scribner's Magazine)
To Catch a Thief: More Adventures of the Amateur Cracksman (May 1901, Scribner's Magazine)
An Old Flame: More Adventures of the Amateur Cracksman (June 1901, Scribner's Magazine)
The Wrong House: More Adventures of the Amateur Cracksman (Sept 1901, Scribner's Magazine)
Chrystal's Century (June 1903, Atlantic Monthly)
Charles Reade (June 1921, London Mercury)

Novels and Short Story Collection
A Bride from the Bush (1890) Novel
Under Two Skies (1892) Short story collection
Tiny Luttrell (1893) Novel; two volumes
The Boss of Taroomba (1894) Novel
The Unbidden Guest (1894) Novel
Irralie's Bushranger (1896) Novel
The Rogue's March: A Romance (1896) Novel
My Lord Duke (1897) Novel
Some Persons Unknown (1898) Short story collection
Young Blood (1898) Novel
The Amateur Cracksman (1899) Short story collection
Dead Men Tell No Tales (1899) Novel
The Belle of Toorak (1900) Novel; published in the US as The Shadow of a Man
Peccavi (1900) Novel
The Black Mask (1901) Short story collection; republished as Raffles: Further Adventures of the Amateur Cracksman
At Large (1902) Novel
The Shadow of the Rope (1902) Novel
Denis Dent: A Novel (1903) Novel
No Hero (1903) Novel
Stingaree (1905) Novel
A Thief in the Night (1905) Short story collection; republished as A Thief in the Night: Further Adventures of A. J. Raffles, Cricketer and Cracksman
Raffles: The Amateur Cracksman (1906) Short story collection; stories taken from The Amateur Cracksman and The Black Mask
Mr. Justice Raffles (1909) Novel
The Camera Fiend (1911) Novel
Fathers of Men (1912) Novel
The Thousandth Woman (1913) Novel
Witching Hill (1913) Short story collection

The Crime Doctor (1914) Short story collection
Old Offenders and a Few Old Scores (Published posthumously) Short story collection

Plays
Raffles, The Amateur Cracksman (27th October 1903) By Hornung and Eugéne Presbrey; first performed at the Princess Theatre, New York
Stingaree, the Bushranger (1st February 1908) First performed at the Queen's Theatre, London
A Visit From Raffles (1st November 1909) By Hornung and Charles Sansom; first performed at the Brixton Empress Theatre, London

Non-Fiction
'Trusty and Well Beloved', The Little Record of Arthur Oscar Hornung (1915) Privately published
Notes of a Camp-Follower on the Western Front (1919)

Poetry
Ballad of Ensign Joy (1917)
Wooden Cross (1918)
The Young Guard (1919)

CPSIA information can be obtained
at www.ICGtesting.com
Printed in the USA
BVHW081930280819
557050BV00023B/1512/P